Scroll Saw Handbook

A Beginner Woodworker's Guide in Crafting
Woodworking Scroll Saw Projects and Designs Plus
Techniques and Tools to Get You Started

By

Kelsey Gibbs

Disclaimer

This publication is designed to provide competent and reliable information regarding the subject matter covered. However, the views expressed in this publication are those of the author alone, and should not be taken as expert instruction or professional advice. The reader is responsible for his or her own actions.

The author hereby disclaims any responsibility or liability whatsoever that is incurred from the use or application of the contents of this publication by the purchaser or reader. The purchaser or reader is hereby responsible for his or her own actions.

Table of Contents

Introduction

Precision is an essential parameter for DIY crafts using wood; this will make for an attractive and accomplished design, and for that, you will need the scroll saw.

Scroll saw; what's it really?

Simply put, a scroll saw is primarily a device for fine cutting. Although the standard material is wood, plastic panels, aluminum panels, and panels made of composite material can be processed just as well on the scroll saw. On the other hand, it is less suitable for thicker beams and boards, and due to the flexibility of the cutting means, the straightness of the cut along the edge is not always optimally guaranteed.

Technically, the scroll saws are basically all the same. The main differences are in the workmanship, resilience, and temple height above all. Scroll saws in the lower and middle price segment usually have a very low bow height. Only workpieces made of thin material, such as plywood panels, plastic sheets or tiles, can be processed on them. Scroll saws with a large bracket, on the other hand, can also be used for beams and squared timber. However, a lot of practice, experience, and a particularly steady hand are required for the precise processing of thick materials. Therefore, large scroll saws are mainly found in the higher price segment.

Without mincing words, for the realization of decorations or for making intricate cuts, the use of a scroll saw is strongly recommended. It is among the tools that offer excellent cutting performance and great precision.

Yeah, at this point, it's understandable that you want to know more about this special kind of cutting saw and what it can really do? Is it a waste of resources or a blessing to your work tools? How about the general usage and other guides to buying and using it properly? Well, these and many other questions are going to be answered in the subsequent chapters of this book. All you need to do now is relax and read through the superiority you are being offered on a platter. You won't be disappointed!

Chapter 1

Saw Scrolling Fundamentals

In addition to talent and training, it is important to have adequate, ergonomic, and professional tools for the cutting tasks to be well performed. This is the case with a scroll saw, which is an essential tool today. All operations are carried out by a blade driven by a vertical movement via an electric motor.

That leads us to ask; what exactly is a scroll saw? Let's take a deep dive.

What is a Scroll Saw?

A scroll saw (also popularly known as a fine grinding saw) is the mechanical variant of the fretsaw. The word Dekupier (the German word of scroll-saw), quite strange at first sight, comes from the French word "découper" and means to cut out or to cut up. Scroll saws are ideal for filigree woodwork such as inlays, wooden puzzles, or candle arches.

Many of us have already had our first experience with the analog model - the fretsaw - in handicraft lessons. The fretsaw can be used to perform fine sawing work, mainly in soft wood or plywood. Figures and other shapes can be sawed out very precisely.

The electric variant is called a scroll saw. It is essentially a work table with a saw frame to which a thin saw blade is attached, which is moved up and down by a motor. The work piece is guided along the saw blade on the table. The saw blade can be easily changed on models with a quick-change system. This is particularly advantageous for interior cut-outs. You drill a sufficiently large hole in the work piece, guide the saw blade through the hole, clamp it, and then saw out the inner piece.

Simply put, the scroll saw is designed as a saw with a handle and equipped with a thin, flexible blade that is mounted below a rigid metal structure. The metal structure is usually U-shaped, and the saw teeth point towards the handle.

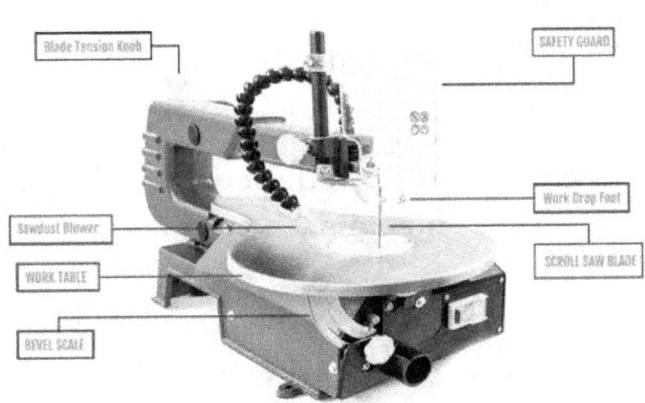

Blade Tension Knob

SAFETY GUARD

Work Drop Foot

Sawdust Blower

SCROLL SAW BLADE

WORK TABLE

BEVEL SCALE

The cutting saw is practical and a piece of comfortable equipment: it allows straight or curved cuts to be made according to each need and can be operated either manually or mechanically. This device can be used on all kinds of material (wood, brass, aluminum, copper, steel, plastic), but it is essential to note that the blade of the cutting saw must be well adapted for each material.

This technique is used to manufacture small curved panels (chair backs, decorative panels, etc.) in cabinet making and, in particular, in making marquetry, violin, and model making. Hence, the scroll saw is by definition a saw capable of sawing turned edges. A scroll saw is an electric saw that typically uses a foot pedal (in some cases) in its operation. It is a reciprocating blade that moves up and down to cut.

Unlike its distant cousin, the bandsaw, the scroll saw does not use a constant blade loop to cut, making it much more flexible and agile when cutting.

This is how it works: it is used to perform filigree and often winding sawing work in the tightest of spaces with high precision. Especially for small shapes, curves, or many points. A typical end product of a scroll saw would be, for example, small-scale wooden decorations, wooden toys, or the well-known rocking arch. Fretwork and inlays are also preferably done with scroll saws. There are countless templates for this on the internet and, especially in America, there are even real associations of hobbyists.

Like most tools are bound to have their benefits and drawbacks, the scroll saw, regardless of how great it is, falls under the same jurisdiction. The uniqueness, however, is that the pros outweigh the cons. Let's take a quick look at the advantages and disadvantages of this machine;

Pros and Cons of The Scroll Saw

The Pros

With great propaganda comes great responsibilities; the scroll saw has proven to be a wonderful tool to woodworkers looking to make precise cuts. However, it doesn't just end there. Highlighted below are some of the advantages of using this impeccable saw;

1. Precise and beautiful cuts are guaranteed

Thanks to its sharp blade and its size, the scroll saw allows cutting in a very precise way. The advantage is that this gives the guarantee of obtaining exactly the desired result, thus avoiding any waste of material. In addition, aesthetics are always in order after each task. On the other hand, it also promotes a curved cut-out.

2. Scroll saws make complex cuts look easy

In addition, with a motorized saw, it becomes even easier to succeed in certain tasks, especially the more complex ones. Indeed, it offers a refined and precise cut, whatever the cutting thickness may be. You just have to put that part on the saw table.

The scroll saw is able to remove a thin slice of material and reveal a design, a marking, or a shape. However, your experience and talent are necessary for a more interesting result. This is all the more important for certain materials such as PVC, which requires more finesse and delicacy.

3. Scroll saws can cut through different materials

Normally, this device is used on wood, plastic, steel, aluminum or soft metals. Also, the saw can perform tight and precise curves. However, you need to make sure that the power and blade are suitable for your material. A blade intended for plastic will not offer a satisfactory result for use on aluminum, copper, or brass

4. Easy to use

In use, the scroll saw is highly appreciated for its practicality. Even if you are not an experienced handyman, you will have no difficulty in mastering the use of this tool.

To operate and stop this device, it usually has an ON/OFF button. The latter is designed to be easily accessible to you so that you can reach it more quickly when needed.

In addition, if you choose an electric scroll saw, you can take advantage of its variable speed drive to increase or reduce the operating speed of the tool. This option is very useful for obtaining the desired level of precision. However, it is also important to handle the device correctly to meet your requirements.

Accentuated above are the many reasons why the scroll saw is very popular in the field of model making and marquetry.

However, if you want to improve your work, you must use a suitable blade. You should know that a blade intended for metal will not have the same effectiveness on wood or plastic. In this way, you will also have the possibility of cutting thicker materials.

The Cons

Irrespective of how great the scroll saw is, it still remains a tool and has the potential to have some drawbacks that can be disadvantageous if proper care is not taken. Highlighted below are some of them;

1. The machine is movable and can cause damage if the body part is misappropriated

Since a scroll saw uses a movable blade to produce intricate cuts in wood or other types of material, this is really the most instantly apparent danger. Since you cannot place your hands or palms directly near the blade, for obvious reasons, the movement of the machine also makes it dangerous.

2. Dusts are inevitable

Ideally, wood cutting breeds dust, and the scroll saw is no exception. In fact, owning its capacity to make intricate cuts, your scroll saw is more likely to cause more dirt and debris than usual. Hence, the uniqueness of proper ventilation comes to play again as failure to comply could lead to health complications. More so, your tool would only get messier and give you more chores to do after work.

3. You might need another tool to cut straight lines

Scroll saws are not designed to cut straight lines. Rather, it's preferred to make twists and curve cuts. Attempting to make straight cuts would only give you poor and less quality results.

Ultimately, always be careful when in the area of an active scroll saw. A trip or a slip could put you in danger. More safety measures will be discussed in subsequent sections.

What Can The Scroll Saw Do?

Let me take the weight to explain some of the common applications of a scroll saw. It can help you learn about some simple scroll saw jobs to make.

Highlighted below are some of the tasks that you can achieve with the scroll saw. However, this list isn't exhaustive but gives you an idea of what you can create with your scroll saw;

- Fretwork
- Inlays
- General cutting of materials
- Cutting of wood, metal sheets, plastic, and more
- Puzzles, Jigsaw and 3D puzzles

- Wood carving
- Intarsia
- Joinery work

If you love making toys, puzzles and kid games, then using a scroll saw is a nice way to craft all of these out. With the excellent blade control and parallel arm extension available on the scroll saw, it's not going to be a problem for it to cut out these fun materials. All you have to do is to simply direct the pieces of wood after making your patterns and then position them under the scroll saw to make the cuts, with a fast cutting motion.

Looking for the perfect tool to make general woodwork and joinery? Then the scroll saw should get that done for you. Should you be looking to make wood joints that look like a dovetail joint or extra strong joint, you can use the scroll saw to make the accurate cut. You can proceed to mark the joint beforehand before proceeding to make the cut. This should give you a clearer means and line to follow to give you a smart cut.

It doesn't end there. For those looking to embrace advanced wood techniques, the scroll saw is one of your best shots. With it, it's easier to make beautiful artwork since the tooth blade is principally removable.

Pre-drilling a small hole in the wood will allow the blade's tooth to flex through easily, giving the scroll saw outstanding flexibility and graciously portraying a high level of creativity.

Other wood techniques, like inlays, are also achievable with the scroll saw. Wood inlays are beautiful floors designed that you see in expensive places and admire. With proper paneling and the use of a scroll saw, you stand an ideal chance to have it within your reach. If you are not comfortable with the basic ones, you can try a more complex inlay procedure called intarsia. This type of inlay involves making intricate and comprehensive patterns and cuts with larger pieces.

Scroll Saw Crafts For Profit

The versatility of scroll saws for making smart and intricate cuts are one of the many reasons why you need to take advantage of it and earn money while pursuing it as a passion.

Don't get it twisted; you need to learn how to manage the scroll saw well, as it's not just a tool to bounce on and understand. Not downplaying its easiness, but you'd have to be a master at making complex crafts on wood with it before you can fully harness its goodness. Hence, the pace for skill and versatility on your part is very necessary. Once you become proficient at handling the scroll saw, here are some sellable ideas you can take on and begin to earn with.

1. Toys

Wooden toys will always hold a particular place in children's hearts since they are well-made and appealing to the eye.

They can be used as a centerpiece in the home or played with by adults and children.

Since most of these items are customizable, they appeal to a broader market when it comes to selling!

Here are some interesting things to do with your scroll saw:

Wood Puzzles

A scroll saw is an excellent instrument for making puzzles since it can create intricate curves. These can be a centerpiece on a table for people of all ages, or they can be used to introduce children to larger and heavier pieces to play with.

Toy Trains and Cars

A scroll saw may be used to make any little wooden toy, but wooden cars, trains, and even planes are highly popular and long-lasting toys.

Doll Furniture

Doll furniture comes with its own market with a lot of buyers for highly accurate and little projects.

Create beds, chairs, dressers, cribs, and a variety of other small furniture items for dolls to put your saw scrolling skills into action.

Toys Houses

Children enjoy prefabricated or buildable cabins and dollhouses, which can be constructed using a scroll saw.

Make animals, humans, and other designs out of any piece of wood for kids to play with. These are the most prevalent wooden toys applications of the scroll saw on the market.

2. Home Décor

One of the most common scroll saw applications is home décor. Beautiful household decorations can be constructed with the scroll saw because they can make delicate cuts. People will want to showcase these in their houses since they generate interesting curves and angles in both wood and metal.

Here are some amazing home décor ideas to try:

Wooden Crosses

Ornately made crosses are lovely additions to any space in the house.

Name Plaques

These can be simply decorated or stand-alone for customized art and can be crafted into bigger pieces of wood or constructed separately with smaller parts.

Clocks

A clock can be made to stand out by putting it in a bigger wood piece , either carved or ornamented.

Decorative Boxes

A scroll saw can simply create modest storage with distinctive engravings and decorations or small boxes for coffee tables.

Topography Art

Topography art is a terrific technique to promote a place while showcasing accurate woodwork by varying in depth to portray mountains and other geographical characteristics.

Wooden Baskets

These can be used to preserve plants in creative designs or as a table centerpiece around the house.

Holiday Ornaments

Holiday ornaments, which can depict whatever design you desire or that others find appealing, can be a popular seller because each year, people are always looking for new additions to their trees. However, profits would be more seasonal in this case compared to other applications of the scroll saw.

3. Furniture

While home décor is more associated with home accessories, scroll saws can also be used to add detail and uniqueness to larger pieces of furniture.

The backing on chairs, artistic additions to table legs, several chests, and other smaller pieces all through the home are all examples of creative uses for scroll saw application.

Many patterns are available on the internet for download, or you can buy a couple of patterns for scroll saw applications to be made easier and give you more ideas for furniture.

There is a market for ornate furniture with numerous embellishments, which can be accomplished using the scroll saw.

If you need projects to start selling, consider the following:

End Tables

For furniture, this is a modest project that you can carve with great detail on the drawers, legs, and trim's top.

Coffee Tables

A bigger coffee table with ornamental designs is a good choice if you're looking for a project that's a little bigger but still follows the same principles as an end table.

Shelving

Shelves are more compact, easier to work with and make excellent decorative furniture for the home. It is less of a financial commitment for both you and the client (compared to bigger furniture).

Wooden-Backed Chairs

On wooden chairs, scroll saw work is hugely common. This is a reasonably simple and elegant piece of furniture that you can make, with many design possibilities.

4. Kitchen Ware

Wooden kitchen utensils are not only functional and usable, but they may also be aesthetically pleasing.

If you like to work with smaller objects on the scroll saw, consider making ornamental kitchen utensils that are fun to build and bring style to many kitchens.

Let's check out some of these kitchen items you can make for profit;

Trivets

Decorative trivets, which hold hot objects, can be used in various ways and are relatively simple to build.

Cutting Boards

With the growing popularity of charcuterie boards for amusement and everyday cutting, a well-designed cutting board is becoming increasingly desirable.

Napkin Holders

A wood napkin holder with unique motifs can serve as a centerpiece in a dining space.

Baskets

Decorative baskets can be used to hold bread or other kitchen items, which can improve the kitchen's aesthetics.

If you choose to work on anything that will come into contact with food, be sure the wood is robust and carefully sanded. Because these things will come into contact with food, paint should not be applied to them.

If you're good at what you do, you might be able to have more long-term work with the client on other jobs. For any contracted job, this is the best possible outcome. You must also be mindful that huge gaps in between jobs may increase your chances of waiting for new jobs and work.

5. Contracted Work

You might be able to get contracted woodwork if you can successfully demonstrate your skills and have the ability to work on bigger projects.

A fret saw is typically used for fretwork, but a scroll saw can be used for ornate woodwork. This work might be used for either interior or exterior woodwork in the home or yard.

A scroll saw can be used to make paneling, garden trellises, ornamental fences, and artistic wood embellishments for someone's home.

The advantage of this type of work is that it might keep you busy for weeks or months at a time, depending on the scale of the project.

6. Teach Scroll Sawing

Having students learn scroll sawing from you can be quite a lucrative alternative. This way, you not only impact but also perfect your skill as time goes on.

To do this, you'd need to have lots of scrolls saws and enough space that can accommodate students. Only then can you begin to source for students around your area and beyond to learn from you.

To increase your chances of having more students, you can recruit students from gatherings such as your local community center, craft fairs, or even schools. However, you'd have to plan a detailed curriculum, tools, and tools to help you schedule your teachings well and try out multiple techniques and use materials.

Upon completing the course, the students would boast of having a formidable skill enabling them to make scroll saw projects.

Chapter 2

Saw Scrolling Tips and Techniques

Using the scroll saw requires skill and practice. In addition, you should also know a few tips and techniques that not only make the scroll saw easier to work with but also make the result look better.

Tips for using the scroll saw; Before, During and After

We've detailed the below tips and techniques and divided them into three parts; before, during and after you're done with your scroll sawing session.

Let's dive into each section right away.

Tips and Techniques to Know Before You Cut

It's completely necessary to check your equipment and ensure they are in the right condition before you cut. However, you'd also have to ensure that your workspace is adequately prepared to manage the task (s) ahead.

Having said that, let's check out some of the necessary tips you should follow before you cut.

1. Confirm that the blade & blade tension is okay

The scroll saw is useless without the blade and when its tensions are not operating at its highest level. Therefore, it's important that you check them regularly before usage to ensure that they can get the job done.

To begin, ensure that you are using the correct blades in the right working condition. If you don't want your work being ruined by a blunt or incorrect blade, then you'd have to be sure about them, always.

Imagine having a damaged output because of bad blades and ruining your hard work. Although the blades aren't expensive, it'd definitely be rather inconvenient for you to handle.

Having confirmed that your blades are in optimal conditions, the next point would be to confirm the blade tension. This can be quite tricky for rookies, but just like operating the machine itself, you'd learn it easily.

Your materials are directly affected by the tension of your blades. If they are loosely installed, it'd be impossible to cut through anything, and if it's too tight, the blades might bend or break completely.

To properly adjust your blade, there are several ways to get that done. For those with a scroll saw that comes with a lever/knob, it'd be easier to find the right tension than those without it. In the latter case, you would have to rely on your sixth sense to find the appropriate tension.

To do this, start by flicking the blade. Doing that would cause it to produce sounds, in this case, a note, like guitar strings. If the installation is tense, it will produce an excessive note and a loose sound if it's too loose.

If you are not familiar with string sounds, you can rely on certain apps that produce guitar strings sounds or if you can, get a guitar within your location to compare sounds. Only when you have perfected this will you get the true ramp. After a while of using the ramp, you'd get used to it and can decide when it's proper to make the right adjustments to your blade.

2.   Dry wood is the best

As much as it's general knowledge that sawing dry wood can guarantee an optimal result, it's still worth mentioning that it is easily forgettable or even ignored.

Sometimes, it might not just be your fault. When your wood is jam-packed in a storage, there are chances it can get wet because of shared heat or when with materials that contain liquid. If this happens, the wood can get damaged and become an occupational hazard if proper care isn't taken.

To deal with that, clean your wood with a dry cloth once you notice it's wet and allow it to dry before using it. This way, your scroll saw can cut through materials without gliding or missing important parts, which can happen when wet.

3. Preparing and positioning the table correctly

Most scroll saws come with an adjustable table that can turn left and right at 45 degrees. However, when making your cut, ensure to have the scroll saw placed at a balanced level without bevel. Once you've done that, it'd be easier to obliterate any inconsistency and note simple observations without issues.

For proper table placement, ensure that the table tones directly with your mid-torso, irrespective of your posture. Only then can will you have a clear view of the table and your work, which is the recipe for excellent cuts.

Also, ensure not to forget about the scroll-saw blades. The blades mustn't be leaning in another direction that's not in line with the table. If the latter happens, you'd have to make adjustments to the blade tension and check for any tears or wear in your blade. If found, replace them immediately.

4. The importance of proper lighting

Having established that scroll saws are used for cutting complex designs and making intricate cuts into shapes and all, it wouldn't be any less better to understand how proper lighting would aid the happening of such quality cuts. Yes, your table and other equipment are set, but you can't make any reasonable cut by just hovering around the table and basing your cuts on assumptions. You need appropriate lighting to see what you are doing.

Many scroll saws usually come with adjustable lights which are either LED or bulbs, but they might not be sufficient. Ensure to tweak your work area to match up with the proper lighting that you want.

5. Sand before cutting

Sanding your wood would only make it smoother to achieve optimal results for cutting any design or shape. However, it's preferred that you do that before cutting.

Not sanding your wood before scroll-sawing would only amount to the material being fuzzy and more difficult to cut. However, doing it beforehand will save your design, its beauty and your time than after cutting.

Tips and Techniques to Know During The Cut

Having discussed the tips and techniques you should know before cutting, it's time to cut and as you know, there are certain tips that'd help you achieve a more quality output. Let's take a look at them;

1. Drilling a hole to the wood can prevent splitting

When sawing, look out for splits. Splitting on your project can jeopardize your project's success, resulting in a long and stressful cut. So, what should you do, especially when working with thin pieces?

You can either drill a hole to the wood to prevent your wood from splitting, or you can place a piece of scrap wood beneath the workpiece you're working on. This will provide leverage and stability for your workpiece and conveniently absorb blade pressure while working, thus leading to a thin piece of wood that wouldn't split.

2. Don't rush when cutting thick pieces

There are times when you'd get overwhelmed with your work, especially when the deadline is close. That notwithstanding, it shouldn't be an avenue to spoil a masterpiece.

When cutting thick wood pieces, time is essential and it's important that you make the best of it. You don't have to rush through cutting them, else you'd make costly mistakes such as having burnt wood or damaging your blades.

Be patient and let it reflect on your work and how you use the scroll saw. You can use the previously mentioned tip by trying the "drill a hole" tip through thin pieces of wood. You can also place a chunk piece beneath your workpiece to help sustain pressure. Since thick wood is the material here, it'd be a no-brainer if you don't drill through until you break the bottom surface.

Having achieved that, turn the wood over so that the other surface faces upward before finishing up your drilling on the side.

3. Don't underestimate the scroll saw

You might have used other saws, but not the scroll saw. Unlike others, this saw doubles up as a heavy-duty tool that has the utmost capacity to complete the project at hand.

You don't need to do much. Simply steer the saw through the wood relatively to the already mapped-out design. You don't and should never have to press onto the blades. Doing that would only result in an accident. Just glide the saw through your design and you'd be done in no time with a perfectly cut result.

4. Cut duplicate pieces in bulk

There'll be times when you'd have to work through several duplicate pieces. Fortunately, the scroll saw is designed in such a way that you can make repetitive duplicate cuts at once. This process is known as stack cutting - a process that's definitely going to buy you more time and save stress.

To make it happen, it's important that you stack up wood pieces that you intend to use, making them face the same direction, all with their best sides. Then, you'll have to hold the stacked pieces together with tape or any other effective process.

Tape is the most advisable and economical process to hold down materials for sawing. Thoyou'd likely achieve better results if you use a tape different from the material being used. In fact, clear packing tape or duct tape would be the best option.

Tips and Techniques to Know After Your Cut

Good news!!! You've prepared for your cuts, learned some techniques during your cut, and you have a masterpiece churned out already. But it doesn't end there. How about after the cuts? Yes, there are things you should do after you are done cutting with your scroll saw. They are highlighted below;

1. **Place a heavier wood on your workpiece to prevent warping**

Not much is needed to be said here, as it's pretty direct. This technique can serve as one that'd help you prepare for a later time. When not properly stored, the probability of wood getting warped is highly probable.

You can start by placing heavier wood on the pieces you intend to use in your subsequent project. This way, the weight of the heavier wood would prevent any form of warping that can impact your wood.

Let's say you weren't careful enough to prevent warping and it eventually happens, it's possible to reverse. All you have to do is dampen the warped piece with a wet cloth and place a heavier material on the warped piece for some time, a week preferably.

With this method, you'll save more money in the long run and preserve your workpiece.

2. **Replace any cut-outs back in place**

When using your scroll saw, there'd be a time when you have to cut from the inside or have some removable parts taken away when designing pieces. You'd have to return these removed parts into the original piece to avoid frail bridges and prevent any possibility of having a potential split.

So then, if there's any need for you to cut out any piece and might not even have a need for it, you'd be doing yourself a lot of good by not keeping it safe somewhere for later use.

3. Using WD-40 will increase the lifespan of your blades

It's unreasonable for you not to have many blades and even duplicate them. Luckily, these blades are quite affordable, and you can easily have them replaced if they become broken or damaged, which is bound to happen as long as you are working with the scroll saw.

On the flip side, once you're done working with the blade, it's recommended that you remove the blade from the saw and spray it WD-40 thin coat. This way, you can protect the blade from getting rust with a longer lifespan.

In case of an alternative, you can always use oil to grease.

Chapter 3

Getting Started With Saw Scrolling

Tools and Supplies

Scroll Saw

You can cut materials precisely with a scroll saw. But what should you look out for when buying such a precision tool?

This section provides you with important information on what to consider before buying your scroll saw.

1. Size

The size of a scroll saw is often referred to as the throat length. It's important to note your scroll saw's throat length. Without it, it'd be challenging to determine the project sizes you can take on. A larger throat length would allow you to accomplish bigger projects, while the smaller one would limit your work rate. So, to make a choice, you'd have to be sure about what you intend to achieve with your scroll saw. Throat lengths of 16-20 inches are a good place to start for a good scroll saw.

2. Arm Type

Scroll saws are designed with three arm types. Each type has its benefits and drawbacks and the decision on which to go for rests solely with you;

a. The most common arm available is the parallel arm. This kind of saw is designed with two arms stretching out parallel to each other with assigned blades at the arm's end area. Should the blades rupture, the saw stops working immediately and the top arm flies out, thus guaranteeing your safety than the rest of the other options.

b. The second arm-type is the C-arm with the iconic 'C' shape. This kind of saw makes a more aggressive cut than the parallel arm and is designed as a single pivot point affixed at the end of the arm. However, unlike the former, if the blade tears, the top part would continue to wobble until you disconnect its power supply.

c. Last on the list of arm-type is the double parallel-link arm. Relatively new to the market, this arm type has a two parallel-arm design that operates only at the tips rather than the whole unit. This kind of arm type functions with less oscillation, making it a high-end choice for the well-to-do "DIYers" with funds to spare.

3. Blade Tensioning

When using a scroll saw, it's critical to make sure the blade is at the right tension for the job. It's not unusual to have to adjust the tension on the fly. I've used my scroll saw several times and discovered that I needed to quickly adjust the blade tension.

There are a few different ways available to change your blade's tension. Some use knobs, while others use simple levers that may be moved into the proper position. Positioning is, in my opinion, the most crucial factor. The tensioning system on a scroll saw can be found in one of two places: on the front or on the back of the scroll saw.

I can't emphasize enough how crucial it is to purchase a scroll saw with a tensioning system on the front. Adjusting the blade's tension on the fly, which is only feasible if the tensioning system is positioned at the front of the scroll saw, will make your life a lot easier.

4. Blade Changing System

The flexibility to change the blade to meet the job requirement is one of the features that makes power saws such useful tools. You can replace your current blade with a more precise or powerful one if necessary. Scroll saws aren't an exception. To make different types of cuts, you can and should change the blade of your scroll saw on a regular basis. Scroll saws, on the other hand, typically have two distinct blade-changing systems. One type necessitates the use of tools to replace the blades. This is certainly a major headache.

The alternative type (which I prefer) allows you to change the blade without using any tools. The sole disadvantage of the no-tool blade changing technique is that the mechanism for exchanging blades can easily break; therefore, be cautious when changing blades.

5. **Blade Types**

Blades for scroll saws come in a variety of shapes and sizes. There are two types of blades in particular that you should be aware of. To begin with, there are pinned blades (or pin-end blades). These blades are thick, allowing them to cut through pieces of wood that are thick. They are also better suited when cutting through wood pieces that are tougher.

The other major type of scroll saw blade is the unpinned or flat plain) blade. You must gently clamp and set the blade tension with flat end blades.

Pinned blades and conventional flat blades both have advantages and downsides.

Pin-end Blades

Pros: The blade is fixed to the proper tension once you lock it. They can withstand big loads and are an excellent choice for cutting hardwood and workpieces that are thick.

Cons: Pin-hole design necessitates that the size of the blade is wider and thicker than usual. For this reason, the pinned blades cannot be inserted into really small holes. This means that the number of scroll saw blades available to you is limited.

Each of the blade types mentioned comes with its subcategories, but the explanations given above, while generic, provide you with the information you require.

The "Choosing The Right Scroll Saw Blade" section below discusses more on these blades.

6. Maximum Angle of Tile

You can tilt the bed to cut bevels or cut at an angle along the workpiece's thickness for several scroll saws.

A blade tilt may or may not be required per the type of job you intend to cut. Check the highest angle at which the job can be tilted in reference to the blade if this is relevant to you.

7. Speed

Most scroll saws will have a variable speed option that allows you to select the ideal speed for your job. If you're just starting out, you can place the scroll saw on a decreased speed to let you figure out how to check things before increasing it up.

The speed of the scroll saw determines the speed at which the saw blade moves. The higher the speed, the faster you can work. However, precise cuts often require a slower speed, since a high speed leads to inaccurate cuts.

8. Cutting Depth

The cutting depth, which is specified by the manufacturers, mostly only refers to wood. A potential scroll saw test winner has a cutting depth of around 50 mm and can use it to saw wood that is up to 5 cm thick. The cutting depth of other materials is usually less (plastic 30 mm, metal 10 mm). If you only want to cut thin wood, a scroll saw with a cutting depth of 40 mm is sufficient.

9. Dust Collection

For capturing sawdust, scroll saws have a variety of systems. A dust blower is standard on most saws. Ensure that the bellow and nozzle are the right sizes and that the location of the blower nozzle can be easily modified.

One of the most unpleasant aspects of using a saw is cleaning up the dust afterward. Connecting a shop vacuum is available on some scroll saw models. Investing in a saw with a reliable sawdust catcher will save you the time and effort of cleaning up after you've finished sawing.

10. Lamp

Another thing to think about is the built-in lighting. You can always fix an exterior light, so this may not seem like a huge concern. Keep in mind, however, that ample lighting must fall on the workpiece, particularly close to the blade, where all the activity takes place.

11. Brand

This is entirely a matter of personal preference. Personally, I like brands such as DeWalt, Excalibur, and Craftsman.

Wood

The ideal wood for scroll saw projects is determined by the nature of the project you are to work on and the purpose the wood is needed for. So let's look at a few popular wood choices first and then factor in other criteria like hardwood vs. softwood, plywood vs. solid wood, and wood thickness.

1. Cherry

Cherry is a good choice because it's easy to cut and forgiving on your scroll saw blade. It's classified as one of the softer hardwoods.

Woodworkers particularly praise cherry for its rich, attractive color. Cherry wood can darken when its exposure to sunlight increases, as well as warp when it dries.

2. **Walnut**

Walnut is a type of wood that falls between cherry and maple. Although not as hard as birch or maple, it's a little harder compared to cherry. For this woodworking material, scroll saws such as the WEN 3920 are excellent.

If you want wood materials without a lot of weight, walnut or cherry are good options.

What criteria do you use to pick between the two? It all depends on your personal choice in design.

Cherry wood offers a warm, rich color that's better suited to holiday decor projects, whereas Walnut has a high-contrast style that's more suited to flooring projects.

3. **Maple**

When compared to other hardwoods, maple is an excellent choice because it is widely available and accessible, relatively inexpensive, and easy to find.

It also has a smooth, even-grain look, making it a popular option among woodworkers. Hard maple wood is selected over soft maple wood only if the project necessitates the use of dense wood materials.

4. Birch

Because birch is a popular cabinet material, you've definitely seen it in a lot of apartments, condos, and showrooms.

Although birch has a curly grain, it's more popular among beginners because it's easier to cut and work with than maple or ash. This wood material can also be easily cut using a scroll saw, such as the high-powered Dewalt DW7788.

5. Ash

Extremely robust and lightweight - two characteristics that any woodworker would appreciate when working on intricate or critical projects.

Hardwoods like ash or maple are excellent choices for detailed design cutting. But keep in mind that ash can be tough on scroll saw blades, so it's not a good choice for beginners.

6. Hickory

For those wishing to accomplish huge scroll projects, hickory is an excellent choice. It's also cheap with the greatest strength-to-weight ratio, making it a very attractive option.

Because of its great hardness, it is tough to cut and will wear out your saw blades considerably faster than most alternatives.

However, given its low cost, you can't go wrong with an inexpensive wood alternative for a large-scale project.

Other Considerations

1. Plywood Vs. Solid Wood

You'd have to decide on the choice that soothes you better when you have to choose between solid wood or plywood. Yet there are appreciations you can contemplate to tweak your choice.

While it's common knowledge that plywood boasts of durability, weather adaptability, waterproof and affordable, solid wood is renowned for better aesthetic beauty and natural glamor. Hence, it points out that plywood is the better option if you are looking for stable and long-lasting designs, while solid wood would fit those who'd prefer to have a more appealing look.

2. Softwood or Hardwood?

Most people would prefer hardwood over softwood. This is because of the softness and brittleness associated with softwood, making scroll sawing difficult.

Making a complex cut with your scroll saw can break your softwood, thereby resulting in you having to start all over again.

This is not saying that softwood is completely useless in the scroll-sawing craft. Of course not. Rather, it's a perfect choice for scroll sawing beginners since there's little resistance to the blade and also pushes them to learn how to cut different shapes and fancy toys.

As aforesaid, hardwood is the better option to handle scroll sawing. Hence, choosing Ashwood and Maple woods would be much better options for professional cutters but challenging for beginners.

Of all the softwood options, the best is poplar. Others are cedar, plywood, or baltic birch.

3. Thickness

The average scroll saws can cut up to 2" thick wood. However, the best thickness ranges between 1/4" to 3/4". As the wood becomes thicker, the harder it would be to make curves and details.

However, a band saw would be a better choice to cut larger inches of wood. Although it'd be challenging to cut out finer designs like the scroll saw, you'd, however, find it easier to cut thicker wood.

That explains why most woodworkers would prefer to use hardwood because the thickness and cuts are usually in the proper range for the patterns to be seen much better. With hardwood, intricate cuts last longer.

Clamps

While some scroll saws include clamps to keep the material in place as you work, others do not. As a result, you'd have to purchase one for yourself. They can also be used to hold down wood pieces while the glue dries.

These clamps are not pricey, based on the model and type you choose. Saw scrolling clamps are the same clamps that are used in woodworking. They are, however, less complicated and easier to use.

Some examples of clamps to use include;

1. G or C clamp: Many woodworkers and saw scrollers are not new to this kind of clamp. These clamps are of the best, known to hold down wood and glued up for easy sawing. More so, there are lots of available samples in this category for you to make a choice from. This clamp's jaw opening ranges from 1-8 inches and can be used to hold down irregular surfaces, all thanks to its swivel head.
2. Pipe clamp: Also known as the gluing clamp, this clamp is easy to operate, especially when it's been used on flat materials. The good thing is, you can

as well use it when scrolling metals. The clamp's jaw is very adjustable; thus, it is suitable for longer projects.

3. Spring clamp: Unlike other clamps, this one isn't attached to anything. It also can't be utilized during sawing due to its small size. This clamp is mostly used to join two or more pieces once they've been glued together. It's shaped like a peg and has a big jaw to keep your wood pieces secured.

4. Bench clamp: This is the most ideal option. It looks a lot like the G or C clamp. You'd have to screw it into a bench or work table. It's mostly designed to hold items on a bench. The height and length of the jaw can also be adjusted.

Spray Adhesive

To bind the pattern to your wood, you'll need to use spray adhesive (a temporary bond spray adhesive works just fine). I normally print a pattern on regular paper, spray the back, wait some few seconds, and then attach the paper to the wood. Various brands are available, which can be found at Walmart, Home Depot, Lowes, and Amazon.

Graphite or Carbon Transfer Paper

Despite its rarity, this approach has some advantages. Let's look at the differences between graphite and carbon paper first.

Graphite is available in a range of colors and can be easily removed from the wood, although it is more expensive.

Carbon paper is a little less expensive, but it is harder to remove off the wood. To eliminate the lines, I suggest using 220-grit sandpaper. Carbon paper is also only available in a few colors; thus, you should only use it on light-colored woods.

Tape one side of your pattern to the wood first when using graphite or carbon transfer paper. After that, tape one side of the carbon or graphite paper down beneath the pattern. This method allows you to position the paper pattern on the wood surface exactly where you want it and inspect your work while drawing.

Finally, trace your pattern with a fine pointed tool like a pencil or pen.

Tip: You may also trace your lines onto the transparent transfer paper first, then use it as a clear stencil in seeing precisely where you want them on the wood surface before you start tracing. One disadvantage of this method is that, depending on your competence, continuous tracing and retracing can somewhat modify the design.

Packing Tape

Packing tape is used to grease the blade, keeps it cooler and prolong its lifespan. It also prevents the wood from burning up. This is particularly the case for cherry and maple woods. I glue the pattern to the wood, secure it with packing tape, and then drill any holes required for my project's internal cuts.

Mineral Spirits

Upon cutting out the project, that's if you applied spray adhesive, you would need to clean the spray adhesive off. You will become frustrated if you attempt to take it off with your fingers.

I've discovered that a 30-second bath in mineral spirits usually loosens the glue enough for it to pull right off. It's possible that a second bath is required. After removing the pattern, I delicately scrape any remaining adhesive with an old toothbrush before allowing it to dry.

Sandpaper

Just like any other woodworking project, you'll need to sand your work. Woodworking is considered to involve 5 percent preparation, 5 percent execution, and 90 percent sanding.

Scroll saw projects may not be as horrible as they appear; nevertheless, you'll need to sand them. An excellent reverse tooth blade, like Olsen, Pegas, or Flying Dutchman, will decimate the amount of sanding required. Following the lines and not having to make sudden modifications upon straying off the line will also help you avoid the need to sand.

That being said, before beginning a project, I usually start with 80 grit sandpaper, working my way down to 320 grit. Then, once the project is finished, I touch it up when and if necessary.

Printer

To print a pattern, you'll need a printer. I've printed using both inkjet and laser printers.

Finish

There are numerous options for finishing your project. But what I personally do just after sanding is to clean the project with mineral spirit. After that, I let it dry before finishing the project with polyurethane. I have, however, tried Danish oil, boiled linseed oil, and other similar oils. Your choice of finish is up to you as the artist.

Apply your finish to your project per the instructions on the finish product chosen. To bring out the grain of the wood, you might also rub it with lemon oil.

Drill Press/ Hand Drill

To make holes for the internal cuts, you'll need a drill press or a hand drill. Because you can't get to an internal cut from the side of your project, you'll need an entry hole to be drilled for the scroll saw blade.

I didn't own a drill press when I started, so I had to use my hand drill. While a hand drill can be used, I damaged a lot of drill bits since it was difficult to maintain the bit straight and the drill bits are small and brittle. Nonetheless, you should get a very good drill press of good quality that will serve you better.

Drill Bits

Drill bits are available at most large box stores, but they are rarely smaller than 1/16th inch. You'll need a hole that's much smaller than 1/16th inch for some scroll saw projects. Mini drill bits will be required for these projects.

The smaller the diameter of the mini/micro drill bits, the higher the number. There are a variety of mini drill bit sizes available; however, the ones I use range from #72 (.0250 inch) to #54 (.0250 inch) (.0550 inch). For example, I generally use a #3 reverse tooth blade. A hole drilled with a #64 drill bit is required for this. The majority of scroll saw supplier websites would include a chart to help you match the blade to the entry hole size you'll need.

Choosing The Right Scroll Saw Blade

Scroll saw blades come in two main categories: pin-end blades and plain-end blades. The main difference between these blades is the number, spacing, and position of the teeth on the blade. Each scroll saw blade has a specific function or material that it is intended to cut.

A plain-ended scroll saw blade has a flat end that attaches to the scroll saw above and below the table. They are most likely to be seen and readily available at any hardware store that sells scroll saw blades. Alternatively, the pin end blades are secured to the saw with a small pin and hook, making replacements more difficult to find.

It is strongly advised that you do not use a saw or blade with a pin end. As a result, I will not cover the pin saw blades here.

Scroll saw blades come in various types depending on many factors. Wood and metal require different blades, as do different material thicknesses and intended cuts. Usually, the space between the blade teeth, called the esophagus, along with the number of individual teeth, determines which projects each blade is best suited for. All blades, regardless of the number of teeth or the size of the esophagus, require the majority of the teeth to face down when installed.

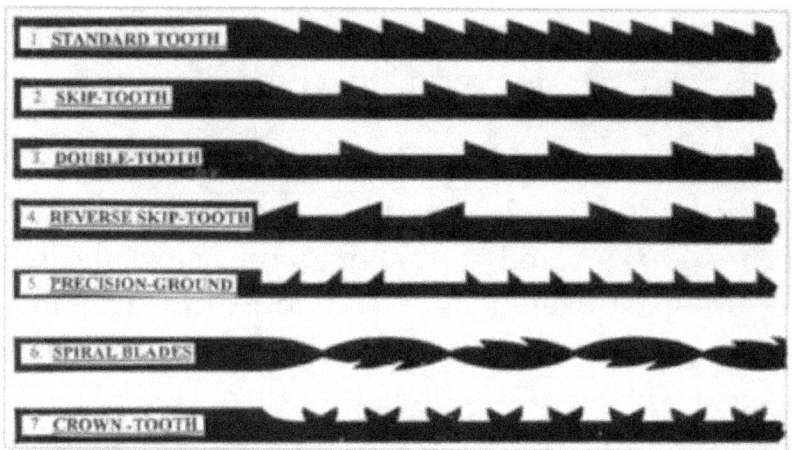

Let's take a quick look at them;

1. Standard Tooth Blades

First on this list is the standard tooth blades. These kinds of blade teeth are similar in size with equal distance apart. Available in only two types; metal and wood, these blades are rather noisy for use. Usually, the wooden blade teeth are larger with more space between the teeth, while the metal blades have less space and small teeth.

2. Skip-tooth Blades

Very much like the standard teeth, the only difference here is that most of the teeth are missing. The space between this blade's teeth is usually distant, thus emitting less noise, giving it an edge for beginner scrollers to harness.

3. Double-tooth Blades

This kind of blade has a wide space between the set of available two teeth. Also known as the "skip-tooth blade," this kind of blade tend to cut slower but more precisely and smoothly.

4. Reverse Skip-tooth Blades

Very much like the double tooth blade except for the available last few teeth beneath pointing upwards. This kind of blade is perfect for preventing wear and tears on wood when making cuts.

To use this, it's important that you set the clamps in a way only two or three teeth are positioned upwards on the scroll table even when the saw arm is placed in an elevated position.

5. Precision-ground Blades

Another type of blade that copies the skip-tooth blade, only that this time, it comes with small teeth that's properly grounded to shape than simply rasped. These kinds of blades are the sharpest when compared to the aforementioned four, and they have stricter and a smoother surfaces when making a straight cut. This type of blade is only recommended for professionals with in-depth knowledge of handling the machine. Amateurs should avoid it for the time being.

6. Spiral Blades

The spiral saw blades are the type that's twisted jointly to ensure that there are teeth around. You don't have to turn your wood in different directions before cutting, as the design of this blade gives you the liberty to enjoy movement autonomy. However, the cuts are usually rough and wider, meaning that they can make tight or sharp cuts. More so, there's a huge tendency of stretching as you use them, making it non-recommended, except for a desperate need.

7. Crown-tooth Blades

These kinds of blades are a novelty to the world of scroll saw blades. Shaped like a crown with space in-between, you can put the blade in any way you want without having to turn it upside down. Although they are slower when cutting than other regular blades, you can easily cut plastic or Plexiglas with them.

Choosing a Blade Size

- Use big blades (higher numbers) when your wood increases in thickness or hardness. For a 3/4 to 1 inch thick medium-hard wood (e.g., walnut, cherry, or maple), a #5 or #7 blade is recommended. Blades with a larger diameter (#9 and higher) are more durable. They're also less prone to fracture under stress and cut more quickly. They're required for wood that's very thick or hard.
- For thin wood, use smaller blades (#3 and lower). When cutting thin wood, these blades cut very gently, giving you greater control. Puzzle cutters often use smaller blades to achieve tight bends, although a #2/0 blade is sufficient for regular scrolling. Select a blade that allows you to cut even the tiniest frets without fracturing every few cuts.

- Select a blade per the stack's thickness while stack cutting. Use a #5 or #7 blade to cut eight 1/8 inch thick wood blanks simultaneously (providing an effective thickness of 1 inch). Use a #2 or #3 blade if you intend to cut four 1/8 inch thick wood blanks.
- Consider how intricate the cuts are. Bigger blades will not fit into tiny frets or cut tight corners. Select the smallest blade that will cut the wood's thickness when cutting complicated designs.

For Beginning Scrollers

For a better explanation about blades and other projects in this guide, it's suggested to use only standard skip tooth. Ensure to buy a few of #3 and #5 skip-tooth and some crown-tooth blades. Also, bigger teeth and thicker blades provide better results on thick or hard materials. Detailed or intricate designs require smaller, more agile blades. When a smooth and precise cut is desired, the number of teeth per inch (TPI) should be increased, although the blade becomes more brittle and prone to damage from increased heat.

As you continue on your quest of learning about the scroll saw, ensure to experiment with other blade types. Go for one that readily fits what you want and can be easily handled. Going all out to get different kinds of blades would only mean you are stocking up without using them.

In addition to selecting the right saw blade for the material to be processed, I also recommend paying attention to the settings on the scroll saw. High speeds on levels 4 to 6 are ideal for processing temperature-insensitive, soft materials such as wood. Whereas low-speed levels of 1 to 3 are better for temperature-sensitive plastics such as acrylic glass or PET.

Scrolling Basics Just Before You Start

Using the saw scroll might be easy to learn, but you've got to admit that it requires some processes to be observed. Failure to do so could cause a decline in your work resulting in poor results. To start on your new scrolling projects, here are some processes to consider which should be used in tandem with all we have discussed in previous sections;

1. **Squaring the Table**

Most of the available scroll saws often come with adjustable tables that give you the liberty to cut through different angles without turning aimlessly. Once you cannot have the table squared properly, you can be sure to have your cuts angled, thereby interfering with segmentation, intarsia, and puzzle pieces, amongst other kinds of scrolling projects.

So how can you ensure proper squaring of the table? Well, you'd have to use a right-angle of a small metal square tool to get that done. Start off by laying the square flat on the table. Make sure it's placed against a properly tensioned and inserted blade. Once this is done, you can adjust the blade's angle to a 90° bend.

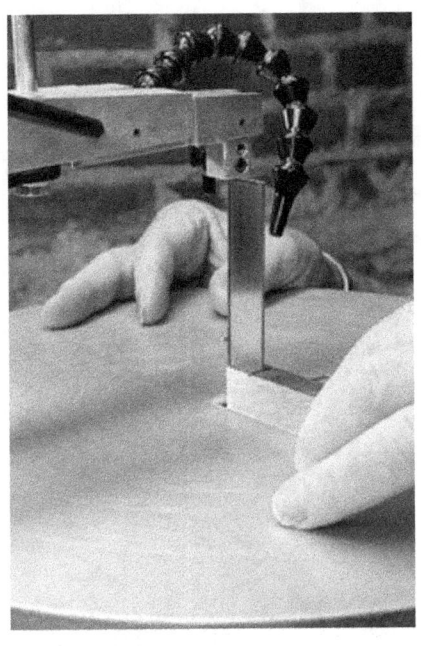

Another option to consider is the cutting-through method. Start off by cutting a scrap wood piece to a 3/4" (1.9cm) thickness. Next, you can ascertain the cut's angle by using a square. Continue to make an adjustment to the table until you have a perfect square cut.

How about using the Kerf-test method? All you need is to get a scrap wood that's as thick as 1-3/4" (4.4cm) and make a cut of about 1/2" (1.3cm) into it. Stop sawing and back out the blade whilst you spin the wood to the blade's back. Should the blade have the capacity to slip into the kerf, then the table is properly squared; else, repeat the test until you are sure that the blade easily slips in.

2. Attaching Patterns

The most common method amongst scrollers when attaching patterns to wood is using a temporary-bond spray adhesive. To get this done, ensure that the wood blank is properly covered with a painter's tape to keep the blade lubricated and make it easier to remove the pattern. Make a copy of the pattern before you proceed to spray the back of the copy of the pattern with the adhesive. You'd have to wait for some time after that before proceeding to press the pattern on the taped wood blank. Glue sticks or rubber cement will do the trick also.

Alternatively, some scrollers use clear adhesive shelf paper. To use this, you will have a pattern piece placed on the table with its shiny side facing upwards. If it's necessary to cut the patterns, do it, after which spray adhesive should be applied to the back, and then the patterns should be attached to the shelf paper.

Another option is the use of graphite transfer paper. Position the pattern perfectly on the wood blank with a sheet of transfer paper placed in-between them. Use painter's tape to hold down the pattern and the transfer paper. Use a red pen to trace the pattern. For dark woods, use light-colored transfer paper. You can also use carbon paper in place of its graphite counterpart to save costs (carbon paper is less expensive than graphite).

3. Stack Cutting

One way to cut duplicate pieces of the same pattern on wood is through stack cutting. This way, you don't have to waste much time replicating duplicate cuts individually; just attach all workpieces together and cut.

To begin with, attaching wood blanks is done using tape. All you need to do is align every wood piece layer together and wrap their edges with a layer of tape. A good example of tapes used for this is the clear packaging, painter, or masking tape.

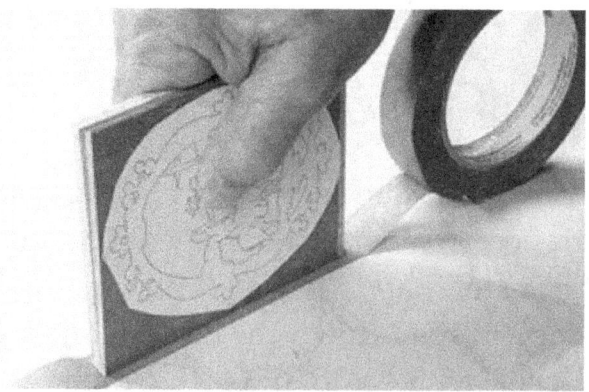

Using hot-melt glue is another alternative. All you have to do is fuse each side of the blanks together with a dot of hot-melt glue.

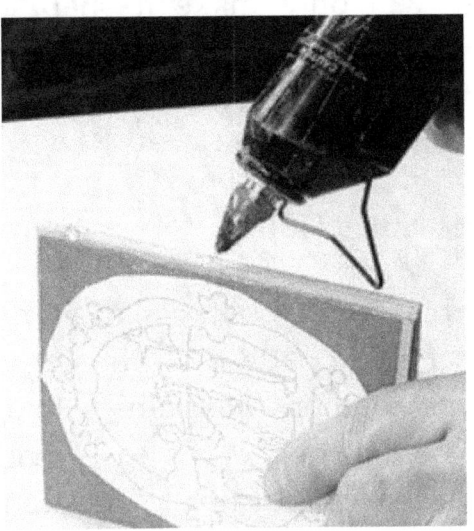

4. Blade Tension

It makes no sense that you'd insert a blade without adjusting the tension first. You should properly adjust the blade tension by clamping both blade ends to their holders. To confirm, use your finger to push the blade and ensure it doesn't flex anything more than 1/8" (3mm) backward, forward, or side to side.

Except that you are comfortable with your blade to wander, you should always ensure that it has enough tension before beginning your cut. Pressing too hard on a loose blade will only make it snap, while a high tension blade will break or pull out from the blade holder. Ensure that you strike a balance where it's neither too loose nor too tight.

5. Blade-Entry Holes

Your pattern blade-entry holes may be marked if you purchase or get a free pattern off the internet. If it isn't, you don't have to bother. All you have to do is place the holes close to a line to be cut to extend the blade's lifespan. However, ensure not to position the hole on the inside corner or curving line. Afterward, a hole should be drilled (drill press or hand drill) perpendicular to the wood blank, making the holes as vertical as they can be. To prevent tear-out on the reverse side of the wood blank, drill into the wood bank and into a block of scrap wood. If there is space available, then use a bigger bit to make threading the blades much easier. If you want to make thin veining cuts, the smallest bit should be used; don't worry, the blade will fit right through it.

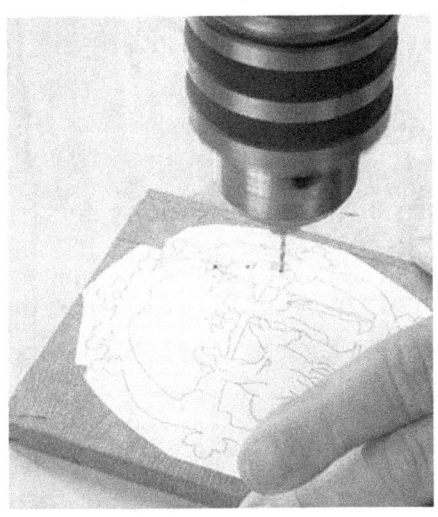

6. Removing Patterns

Wiping off with mineral spirits will ease the stress of removing the leftover adhesives on your wood. If you can't get mineral spirits, you can trust the commercial adhesive removers to do the job well enough.

Staying Safe When Handling The Scroll Saw

Even though the scroll saw is a very safe tool for beginners, you should ensure that your safety is always your top priority while working in the workshop, and understanding the safety routine is critical to avoid any mishaps.

Below are a few safety tips to adhere to:

Scroll Saw Safety Requirements

- Make sure your scroll saw is securely fastened to your workbench or tabletop.
- When making any adjustments, conducting maintenance, or changing the blade, ensure the power is turned off and the cord is unplugged.
- Use the correct blade for the cuts you intend to make.
- Make sure the blade's teeth point down and forward toward the table.
- Make sure the blade tension you are using is correct.
- Never start the saw before you've cleared the table.
- Start the saw scrolling machine only after all of the handles have been locked.
- When the scroll saw is running, avoid reaching under the table.

Workplace Safety Requirements

- Maintain a perimeter of 2ft around the scroll saw clear of debris and people.

- While operating the scroll saw equipment, you must also wear safety eyewear like protective goggles to avoid eye injuries from wood splinters and dust suddenly flying off.
- Arrange your surroundings so that, for example, the scroll saw on the table is at the right height for you.
- Scroll saws emit a lot of dust, so make sure you're working in a well-ventilated location. If you use a suction function, adjust the suction tube to collect chips and dust optimally. You might also need to put on a mask or respirator.
- Ensure there is good lighting in the workplace to avoid working in the dark. Some of the best scroll saw models have enclosed lighting for the workplace in the form of a halogen lamp. While for other scroll saw devices, you may have to buy such an option separately.
- Additional hygiene measures in your workplace must be implemented, such as regular cleaning of the floor and the walls of the workplace using a suitable industrial vacuum cleaner with an absolute filter (no blower or broom which disperses the dust in the air) and the frequent evacuation of sawdust from the workplace.

- Make certain that no loose jewelry, clothing, or hair gets in the way of the saw.

Operational Safety Requirements

- Before turning on your saw, make sure it's in good working order.
- The workpiece must lie completely on the table. This way, you have a precise guide, and the workpiece cannot suddenly break out under the pressure of the saw blade.
- Your fingers will always wander repeatedly towards the cutting surface to guide the workpiece. So, ensure to maintain a safe distance between your fingertips and the blade and never put your fingertips in direct contact with the blade. If you slip, you don't want to lose a finger.
- When you start the saw, the blade should not be in touch with the wood.
- Use the appropriate speed for the wood you're cutting and the type of cutting you'll be doing.
- Make relief cuts before cutting any sharp or lengthy curves.
- Stop the scroll saw and allow the blades to stop moving before attempting to remove any little scraps of wood off the table.

- If the wood doesn't have a flat bottom, don't try to cut it.
- After you are done with the scroll saw, let go of the blade tension. The blade will be less stressed as a result of this.
- When you're through, wipe your table with a bench brush.

Scroll Saw Maintenance Requirements

Since scroll saws are cutting devices, they produce dust that can get stuck in the scroll saw mechanism. That is why regular cleaning and checking of a scroll saw is an essential part of the scrolling process. The usual care and maintenance steps for scroll saws are as follows:

- Visual inspection: It is advisable to check your scroll saw thoroughly before each use. Before usage, make sure that all housing screws are firmly seated and check the device for backlash in all joints and any damage. The two minutes that you invest in tightening all housing and joint screws will pay off in the long run.
- Compressed air cleaning: Part of the resulting dust finds its way inside the scroll

saw machine. You should never take the machine apart to clean it from the inside. It is entirely sufficient to blow them out with compressed air along the ventilation openings. This will prevent the sharp air pressure from causing damage inside the machine.

- Exterior care: Clean the outside of the machine with a damp cloth. A light soapy water is sufficient as a cleaning agent. After wiping it, rub or blow the machine dry.
- Maintenance: All other maintenance checks, such as greasing joints, should be performed per the operating instructions of the scroll saw machine. The careless use of lubricants and solvents can damage the machine.

A Short Message From The Author:

Hey, I hope you are enjoying the book? I would love to hear your thoughts!

Many readers do not know how hard reviews are to come by and how much they help an author.

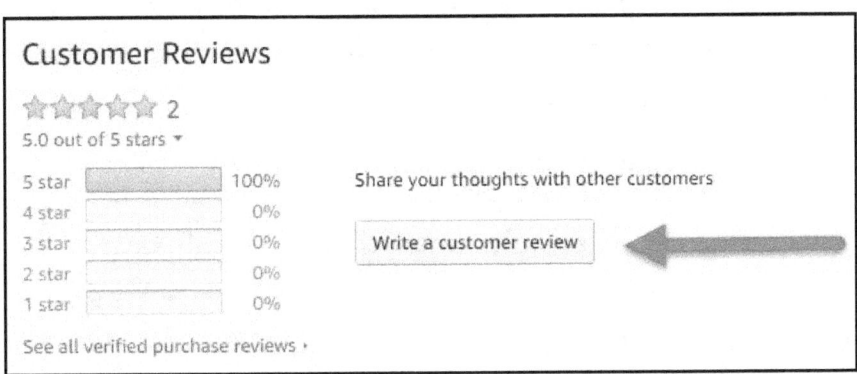

I would be incredibly grateful if you could take just 60 seconds to write a short review on Amazon, even if it is a few sentences!

>> Click here to leave a quick review

Thanks for the time taken to share your thoughts!

Chapter 4

Saw Scrolling Project Ideas

So far, we've ascertained that the scroll saw is one of the most fun and easy saws to use. Of course, you won't be using them to build a garage or patio, but scroll saws come in very handy for decorative projects and creating unique gifts for friends and family.

In this section, we will be looking at a couple of easy project ideas you can take on with your scroll saw.

Dinosaur Puzzle

You can make wooden dinosaurs to show your children as part of what they love to read or watch. All that's required for you is to get creative.

Materials

- Your choice of wood. Walnut was used here
- Drill press or hand drill
- Scroll saw spiral blades
- Scroll saw

- Spray adhesive
- Butcher block oil finish
- Your choice of pattern for your scroll saw
- Sandpaper

Additional Materials

- Orbital sander sandpaper
- Table saw or jigsaw
- Portable drill bit
- Power planer
- Dewalt orbital sander

Instructions

The pattern

1. Ensure to surface the wood

Surfacing your wood is an optional step. However, if your choice of wood is a 1 x 8 oak piece that you got from a large box store, then it's likely surfaced already. However, if it isn't, you have to surface the board's sides until it's smooth.

2. Glue your patterns down

Use a spray adhesive to hold the pattern to the wood.

3. **Cut out the bulk material**

Here, remove as much material as possible. My table saw was used to cut as close to the dinosaur's outline as I could. A jig saw can also be used for this.

4. **Begin to cut**

Moving on to the fun part. With you having inserted your spiral blade into the scroll saw, you can start cutting out the dinosaur's outline of the dinosaur. For optimal results, ensure to further push the piece from you in a similar direction. What this means is that you'd have to continually rotate the piece as you cut to push them further away from you until you've cut out a magnificent piece.

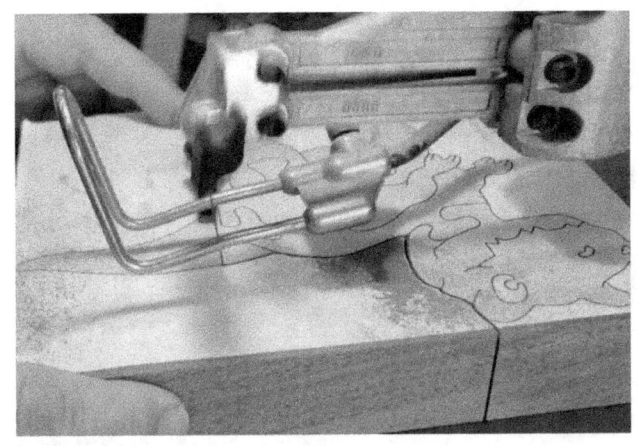

5. Cut out the individual parts

Cut out the individual parts until they're all separated.

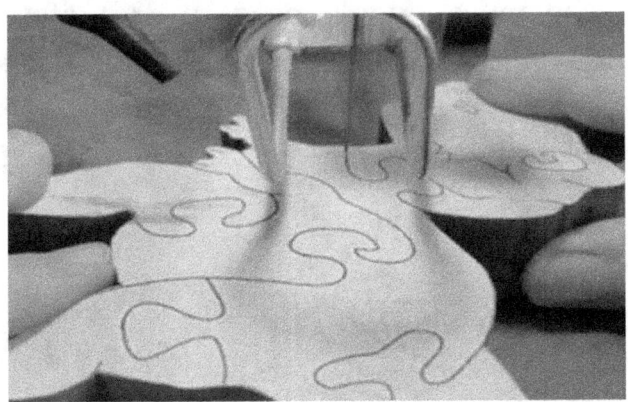

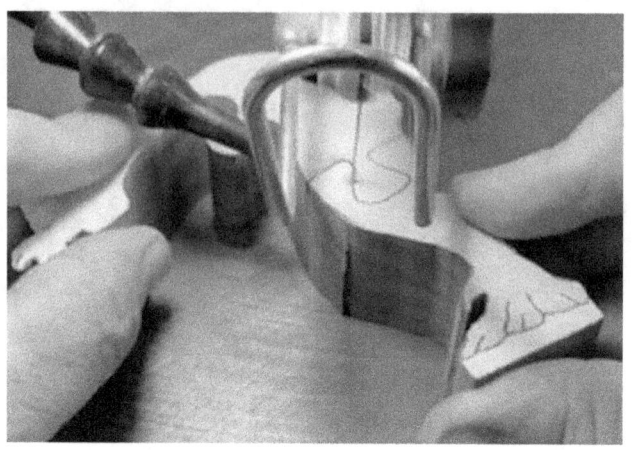

6. Drill holes for interior work

If your pattern calls for any cutouts to be made on the inside of the pieces, you'll need to drill pilot holes. I used a 1/8" drill bit because of how small it was to fit the inside of the outline. Basically, you'll only need a big enough bit to allow you to drive the spiral blade via the wood in the next step.

7. Cut out holes for the interior

Remove the blade's top section, run it through the workpiece, and then reconnect it to the scroll saw. You can now finish cutting out any remaining internal holes.

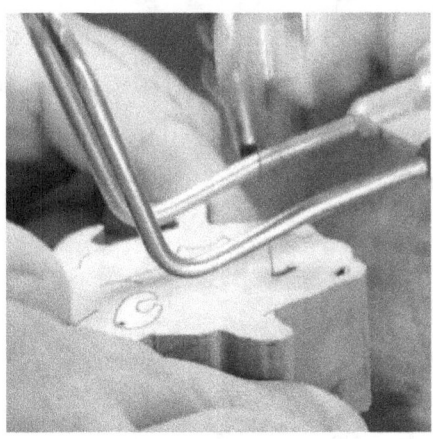

8. Sanding

I began by sanding the rough edges left by the scroll saw on my pieces by placing an 80 grit sandpaper on my workbench.

The scroll saw pattern paper was then removed using the disk sander. You can do this by hand, but if the adhesive does not cling as well as mine did, the paper may lift off.

Finally, each piece's edges were sanded to remove any sharp edges. I also used 120 grit sandpaper to sand down the whole piece.

9. **Finish application**

Well, since this is a project that kids would most likely handle, it must be safe enough from the sharp cuttings and chemicals. Using the Butcher Block Conditioner finish would be perfect since it's safe enough to be used for food.

Begin by having liberal amounts of the finish applied to every part of the workpiece(s) by using your hands to rub it in. Accessing the inner parts might prove challenging, so the best shot for you is to have a toothbrush to access the inner parts. Once you've successfully applied it over, clean off the excesses with a rag or towel.

 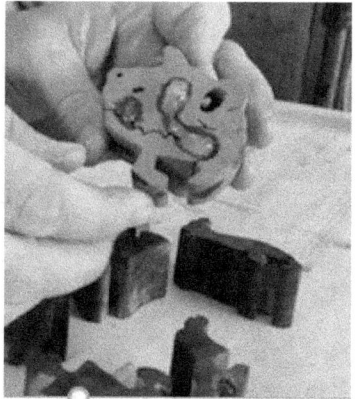

You've done well up to this point. Now it's time to hand it over to your little one to learn and play with them

Utensil Trivet

A trivet is like what you need to place a hot pan on. This project idea is a creative design that resembles a burst of forks, knives, and spoons.

Materials

- Scroll saw
- 12"x12" slab of your desired wood
- Transfer paper
- Utensil design pattern cut from vinyl
- Sandpaper

Instructions

The Pattern

1. Set the design pattern (faced down) on the adhesive part of your transfer paper, straighten and flatten it out. After that, remove the thicker backing and push the entire sticky object onto your desired wooden surface, making sure it's aligned at the center.

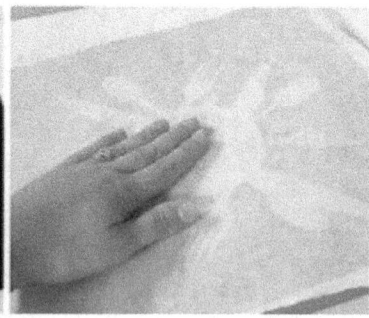

After that, take out the transfer paper to reveal your stencil, which is now firmly secured.

2. Trace the pattern. I considered tracing this design with a pencil and then ripping off the vinyl, but I realized that leaving it on and cutting it with my scroll saw would be easier. But first, I turned it over and cut off the excess vinyl that overlapped the sides using a Xacto knife.

3. Then cut your design right away using your scroll saw.

Once you have the bulk of the workpieces cut out, go ahead and remove the little crevices left off.

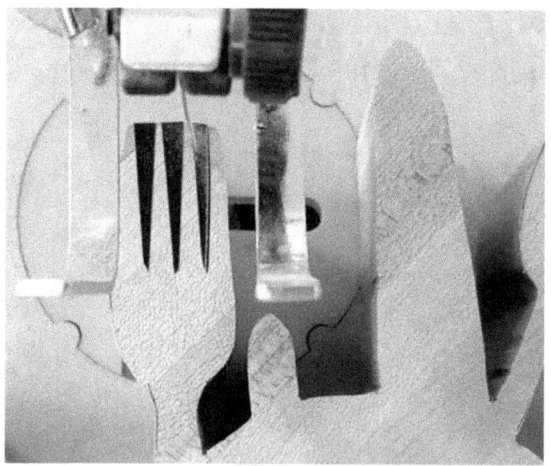

4. Simply sand the edges with 220 grit sandpaper to finish.

Basket Bowl

Who would have thought it would be possible to make a bowl with a scroll saw - from a simple small plank of wood? I hope you will like the result and inspire you to create your own model.

Material

- Scroll saw
- Your preferred wood choice
- Printer

- Drill bits
- Drill press or hand drill
- Spray adhesive
- Sandpaper
- Finish

Additional Material

- Jigsaw
- Wood glue

Instructions

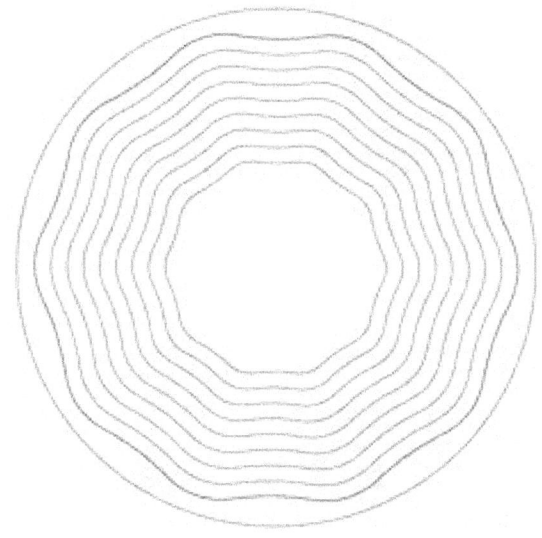

The Pattern

1. Scale the above pattern to the desired size of the basket, print it, and cut it out.

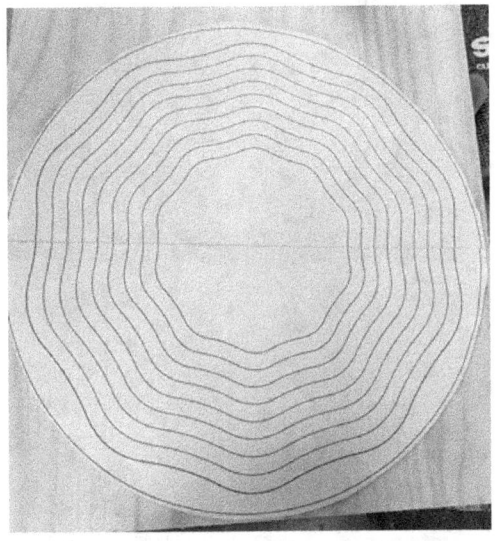

2. Glue the pattern cut out from step 1 onto your wood board, or preferably, use a spray adhesive.

3. Cut the board to size. With your jigsaw, cut the board into manageable sizes; although a scroll saw can be used, a jigsaw is faster and easier.

   Then cut along the outside circle with the scroll saw.

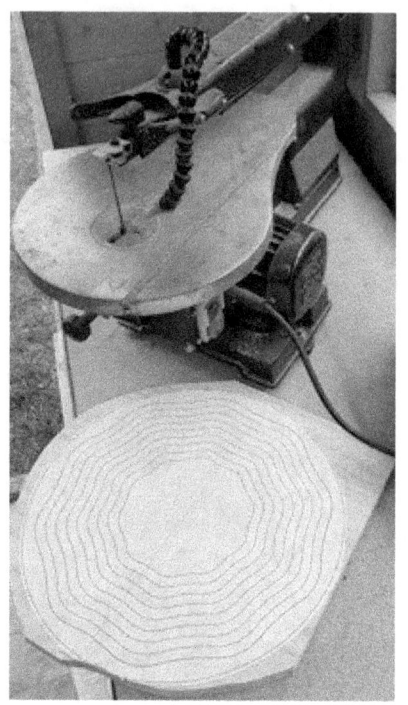

4. Drill holes as small as possible (lesser than 5mm) to allow your blades feed through.

5. Feed your blade via the entry hole, cutting along the lines with your scroll saw. To guarantee results, start off slowly and apply pressure gently to allow the blade to cut through well enough. You might find it challenging to make curves, but you should be fine with the slow and steady method.

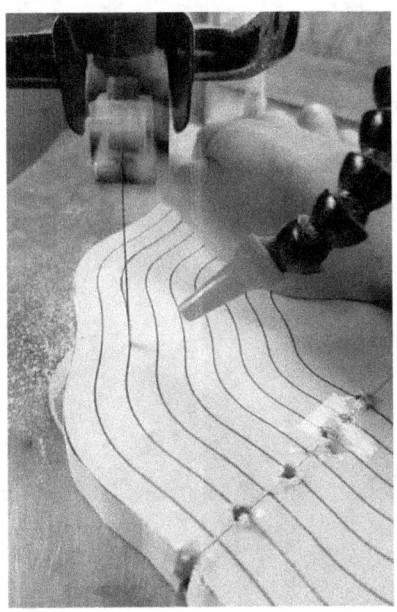

6. After cutting all the pieces out, you can arrange them as you want; you can vary the grain orientation or the style of the bowl/basket.

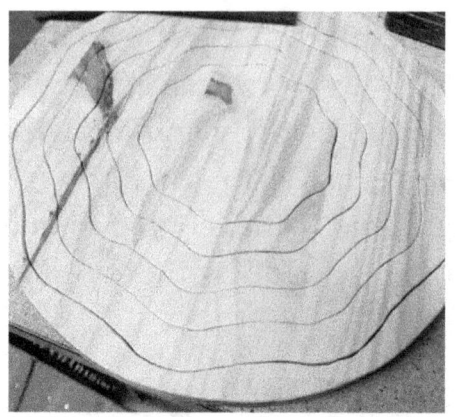

7. Fill up drilled holes. Now, if you used a pin end blade, your entry holes will come out large, and you have to fill up the hole to hide them using a wood filler, but if you used a pinless blade, then there is no need to fill up the holes

8. It's time to sand. Sanding required some time to get the sides smooth, but it is worth the time and effort because it would be much more difficult once it was glued up. Parts of this were done using a Dremel, but it could also be done by hand sanding. A coat of cellulose sanding sealer was applied and allowed to dry; because this elevates the grain, I went back over the pieces with a Scotchbrite pad. After smoothing everything out, I dusted it all down in readiness for gluing.

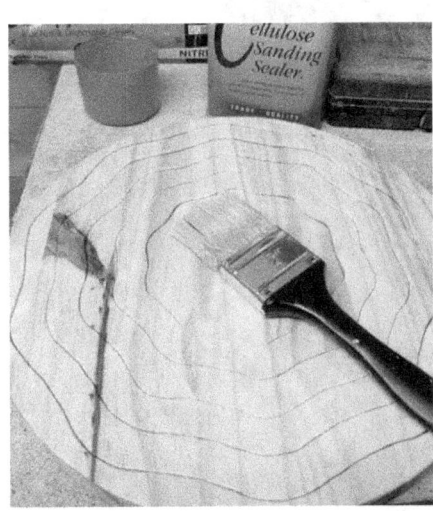 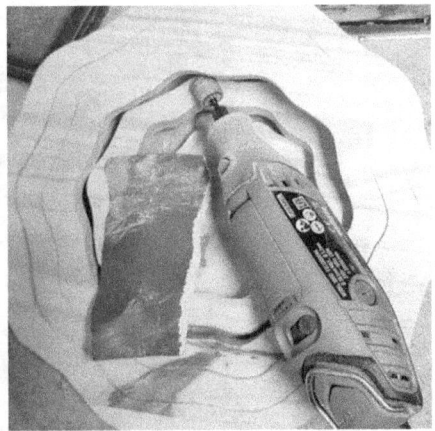

9. Prepare to glue. I put a dab of glue on the edges that needed to be bonded and clamped them

around each other, two at a time. Once dried, I then glued and clamped the three sets together.

I cleaned up any extra glue that had hardened, then used sanding sticks to sand small detailed sections. I used and shaped some lolly sticks into a point, gluing them to the backside of some sandpaper. Then I cut them out with a utility knife and began removing the glue.

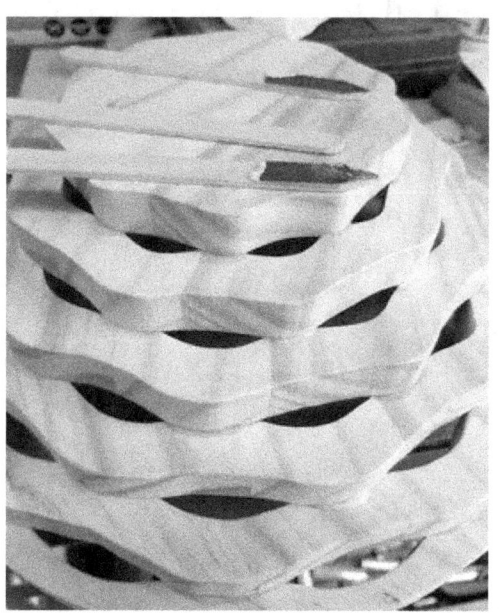

10. Apply your finish.

Applying a finish of your choice is the final step to completing your wooden bowl. You can apply a food finish to make it suitable for storing fruits. Ensure to apply it lightly, so it doesn't take longer than usual to dry up.

Christmas Ornaments

Materials

- 1/4" MDF wood scrap
- Scroll saw
- Drill press or hand drill
- Drill bits
- Printed shapes
- Sandpaper
- Spray adhesive

Additional Materials

- Adhesive shelf liner film/ contact paper
- Gold spray paint

Instructions

1. Apply your shelf liner paper or contact paper to the top of the MDF wood scrap you will be cutting from. The spray adhesive you'll use to attach the design for cutting will be protected by this.
2. Search the internet for free Christmas ornament pattern, then proceed to cut out the designs precisely, using spray adhesive to attach them to the contact paper.

105

Then cut out the shapes with your scroll saw

3. Each shape should be cut out. Drill small holes in every area while cutting inner areas, then re-attach the blade into every hole drilled for each area. Remove it when you have cut out that small area.

Drill small holes in each inner area

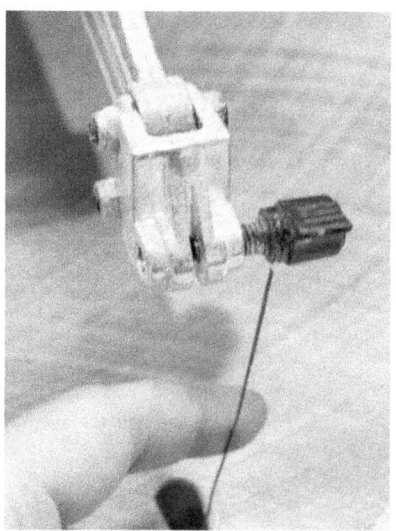

Detach the top of the scroll saw blade

Reinstall the blade in the scroll saw after inserting it into the small hole. Cut the inner area out. Repeat

Cut out the remainder of the design

4. Take off the contact paper on the cutout design

Then sand the individual cutout design on the front and any rough spots with 220 grit sandpaper.

5. Lightly cover the shapes with a good metallic gold spray paint. When the first coat has dried, apply a second coat. And you are done!

Leaf Coasters

Materials

- 10" x 24" scrap plywood
- Scroll saw
- Sandpaper
- Finish

Additional Materials

- Pen for tracing
- Scissors for cutting out design pattern
- Jigsaw or circular saw

Instructions

The Pattern

1. Scale the monstera leaf pattern down to around 5". Print it out.

I then used scissors to cut it out and use it as a model for my first leaf. (After cutting out the first coaster, I used it as a pattern to trace the remainder onto the wood).

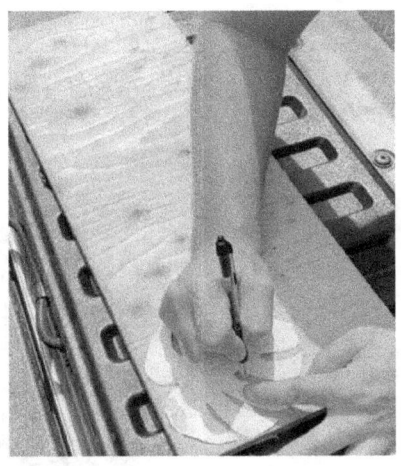

2. Cut the monstera leaves apart

I cut the plywood to the required size using a jigsaw or a circular saw before starting to cut with the scroll saw. It is considerably easier to maneuver when done like this.

With the scroll saw on a medium-speed setting, I then cut out all of my monstera leaf coasters by following the lines.

3. Time to sand

I started sanding when I finished cutting out all of my coasters. I used a coarser grit and then a finer grit paper with my mouse sander. I used a 120 grit sandpaper on both sides of the coasters and the edges, and then a 180 grit sandpaper on the top side for a smoother surface.

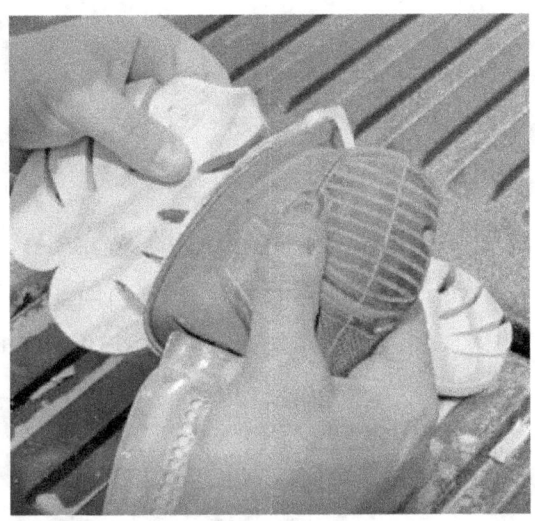

4. Stain and waterproof

Here, I used an aqua-colored water-based stain for my finish. You are free to choose your preferred color.

I sprayed a coat and then used a rag to rub it in thoroughly before wiping away the excess.

This method was repeated for two coats of stain and I was pleasantly surprised by the results. Below is the pattern I got when the stain worked its way into the natural grain.

Finally, I applied three coats of spray-on polyurethane to each coaster for a durable, waterproof finish.

Illuminated Clock

An economical solution to decorate your own DIY clock! Why? The personality! Like most DIYers, it's always more fun to create your own version of what could be a utility item. And yes, we still need fancy clocks.

Materials

- Spray adhesive glue
- Drill
- Drill bits
- A large piece of plywood
- Scroll saw

Additional Materials

- An analog clock

- Circular saw
- Styrofoam
- Movable lamp
- Pencil
- Hot glue

Instructions

1. Trace

On the plywood, trace the surrounding of the clock. You can use a pen instead to make the lines thicker and more visible

2. Cut

It's time to cut. Use your scroll saw to cut the clock's surroundings.

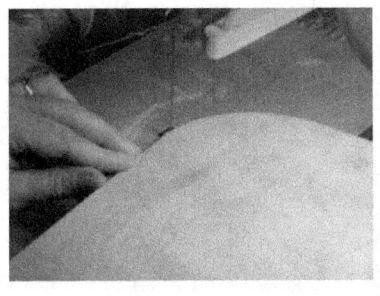 

3. Glue

Lightly apply spray adhesive glue on the surface of your analog clock.

4. Drill and cut

At the end of each digit, drill a hole. Insert the circular saw across each hole, then cut it off. A jigsaw can also do the job

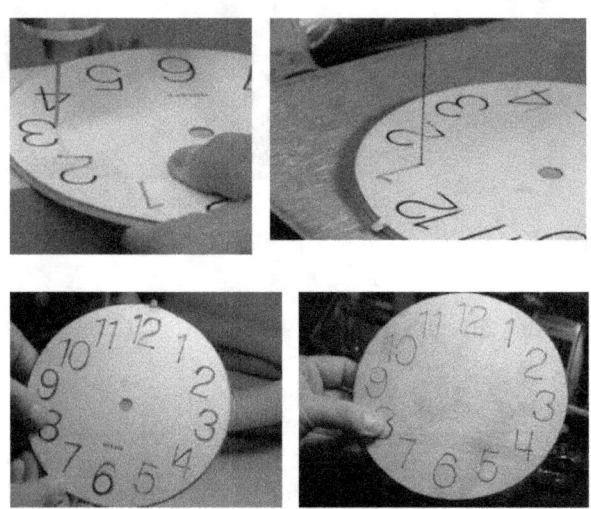

5. Attach to light

Assemble all parts (the light, the movement of the clock, the frame, and the clear plastic piece).

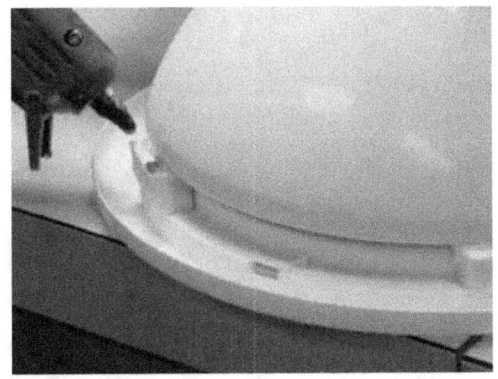

You are done!

Music Themed Shelf

Materials

- Wood (preferably cherry)

- Patterns
- Spray adhesive
- Finish
- Sandpaper
- Drill bits
- Drills
- Scroll saw

Additional Materials

- Keyhole hangers (to mount the shelf)
- Jigsaw
- Wood glue and nails
- Air nailer
- Scissors

Instructions

The Pattern

1. Print and cut out your pattern to shape with scissors, then apply on the wood using spray adhesive

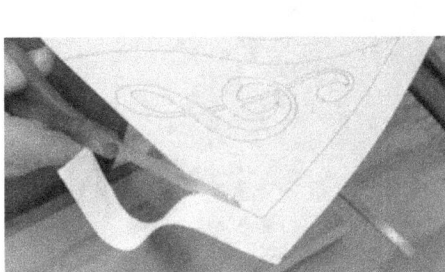

2. With the jigsaw, the outside section was cut off. Then I drilled all of the scroll work's starting holes.

3. For the scrolling, I inserted the blade into one of the holes drilled earlier and reinserted the blade

to the scroll saw's upper arm. The pattern is removed once the scroll work is completed.

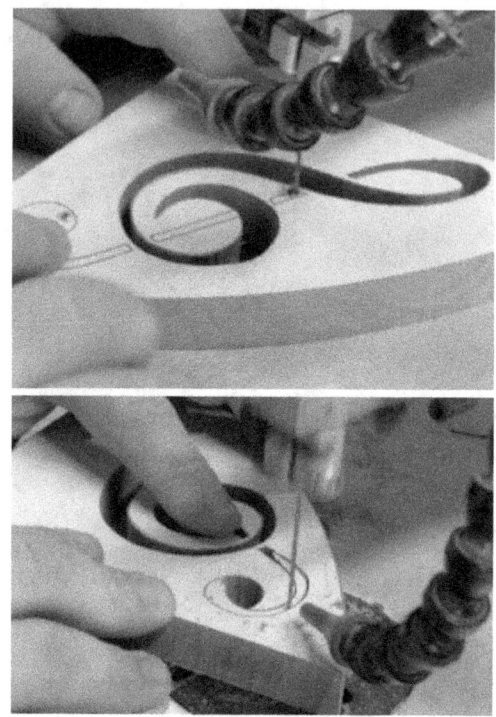

4. To mount the design, a set of keyhole hangers were used. I screwed the hangers into the shelf to hold it into place. The shelf's top base was built from scrap wood left over after cutting out the designs (brackets).

5. Attach the design. I chose a simple technique in attaching the brackets because I knew what

would be on the shelf and the location it would be hung. They're held together with wood glue and brad nails. Wood glue was applied underneath the shelf base, the bracket was installed, and brad nails were driven into the base from the top.

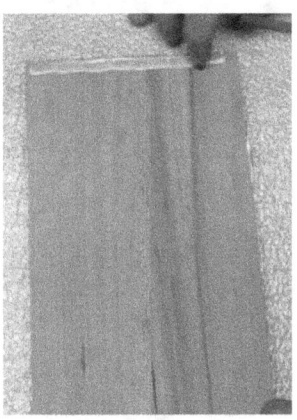

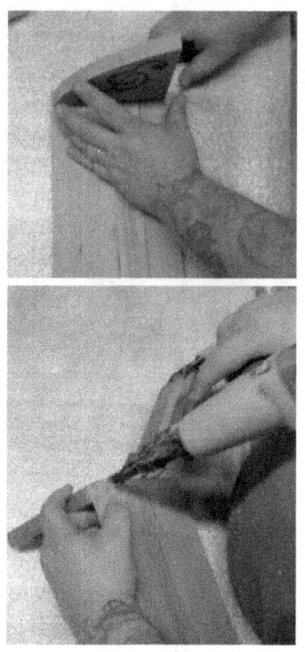

6. Finishing. I sprayed the entire shelf with spray polyurethane because the cherry wood was so good. It took some layers of coating with some little sanding in between to get this done.

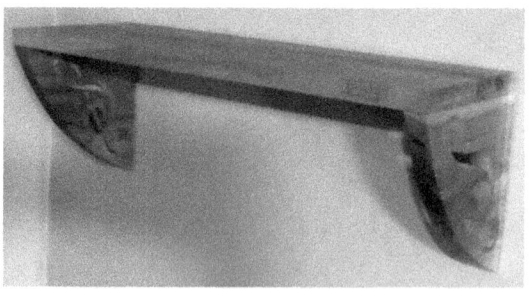

KeepSafe Box

The keepsake box is a great idea for storing things with great sentimental value. Each box is different: some are colorful and personalized, others simple and sober. Think about your style and consider how important it is to you to keep these memories. Also, consider whether you will create it for yourself or for a friend.

Materials

- Cherry or maple wood piece
- Box template
- Adhesive spray
- Scroll saw
- Hand saw
- Drill
- Drill bits
- Finish

Additional Materials

- Sander
- Wood glue
- Trim router
- Hot melt glue

- Handsaw

Cutting List

- (1 wood piece) 1/4 inch thick x 5-1/2 inch wide x 8 inches long
- (1 wood piece) 1/2 inch thick x 5-1/2 inch wide x 16 inches long
- (1 wood piece) 3/4 inch thick x 5-1/2 inch wide x 16 inches long

Instructions

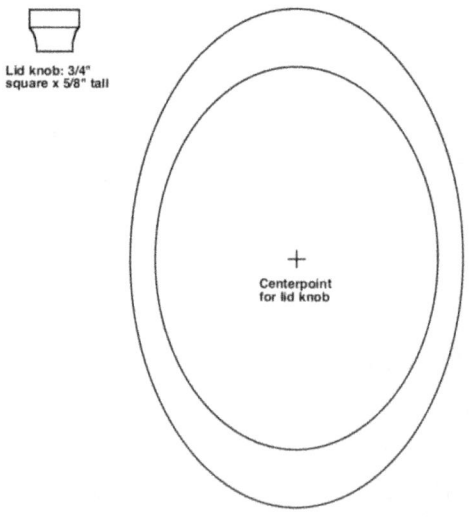

Lid knob: 3/4" square x 5/8" tall

+
Centerpoint
for lid knob

Box and Lid Template

127

1. Print off the template for the box and lid and use spray adhesive to attach it to your wood piece of 1/4-inch thickness. Trim away any extra paper.

    Cut the outside oval to size on your scroll saw, or better still, you can use a jigsaw, then drill a small starting hole on the inner oval's layout line. Make the hole big enough for a scroll saw blade to fit through. Cut out the inner oval with care; you will need the two ovals for the finished piece. Smooth the bigger oval's cut edges to be used as a template.

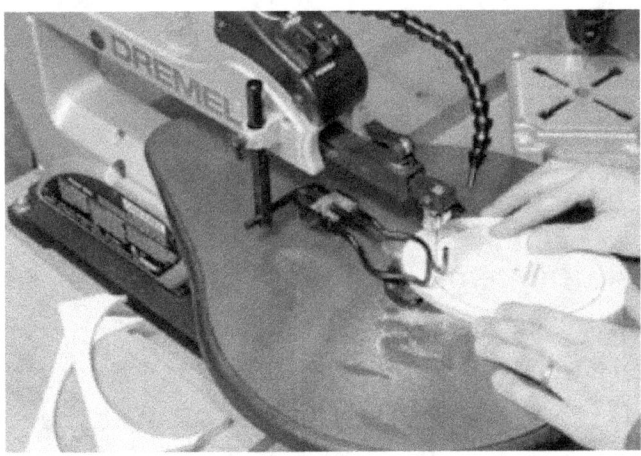

2. Use the template to trace two ovals onto a 1/2-inch wood piece. Only trace the perimeter. Then, on another 3/4-inch wood piece, trace the inner

and outside sides of the template. Draw two copies of the shape. Cut off the four ovals and the inside cutouts to make the top, bottom, and center two layers of the box. Cut them at around 1/16 inch outside the lines of the layout so as to sand these parts to their final shape.

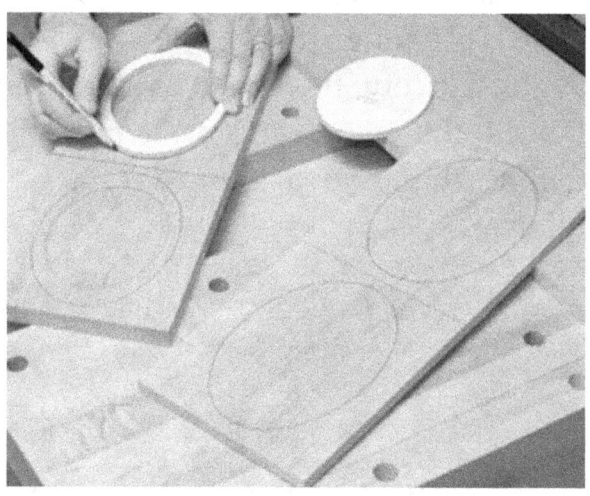

3. With the template wood piece on top, glue and clamp it alongside the center two (3/4-inches thick) layers. After the wood glue has dried, sand the wood piece's inside edges to fit the shape of the template. The exterior edges should not be sanded yet. To make this sanding task go faster, utilize a drum sander or an oscillating spindle

sander inside your drill press. Hand-sand the inside of the box for a smooth finish.

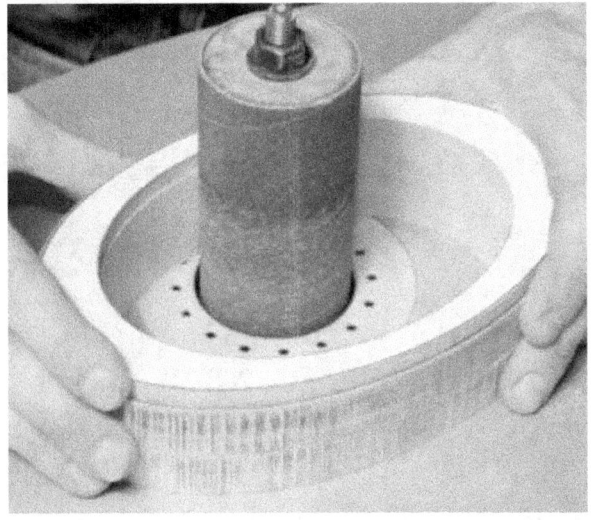

4. Finish sanding and gluing one of the 1/2-inch thick ovals to the base of the box blank. You can now improve the outside look of the box by sanding the layers until they fit the template's top. The best tool for this job is a disc sander.

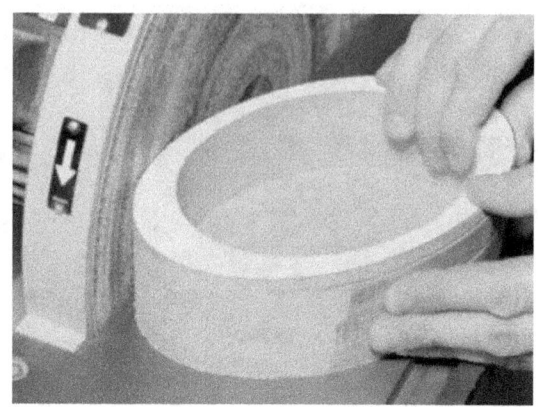

5. Use a few dabs of hot-melt glue to temporarily attach the remaining 1/2-inch thick oval to the box's top. It will be used to cover the top of the box (box lid). Ensure the big lid piece equally overhangs the box's outside sides.

6. Sand the lid's edges until they fit in with the rest of the box. You can use a disc sander or a smaller detail sander. After that, sand the lid, bottom, and face of the box up to 150 grits.

7. With the lid secured to the box, use a trim router and a 1/2-inch roundover bit to smooth the rough edges. To avoid tear-out and burn markings, remove the waste in successive passes of increasing depth. Sand the routed edges to fit in the curved transitions, then smooth all of the boxes's outside surfaces using 180-grit sandpaper.

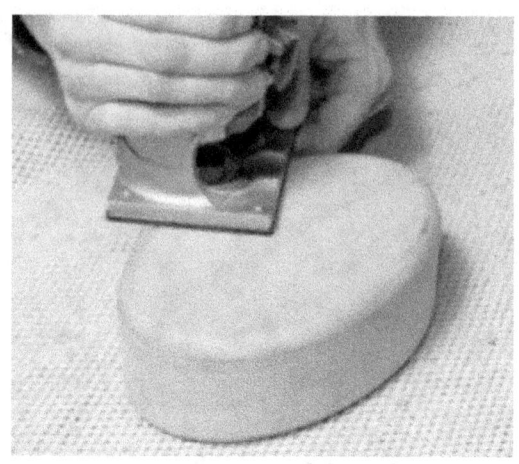

8. With a rubber mallet, carefully tap the lid off from the box. Ensure this is done on a padded surface to avoid damaging the lid!

   Sand the box's rim to remove the paper pattern. Then, sand the paper off the inner oval cut out in the first step 1; smoothen the edges. To enable it register on the box, this piece will become the inner layer of the lid. Trace the position of the inner layer on the lid using a separate photocopy of the paper pattern. The lid sections should be glued and clamped together.

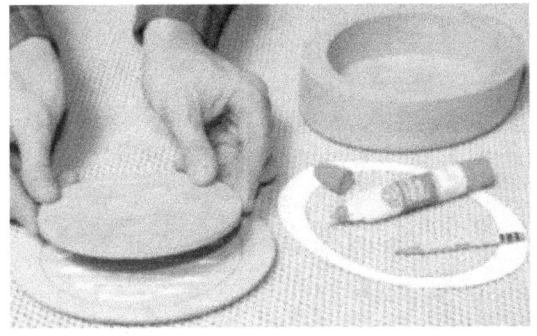

9. For the lid of your box, you can use any type of hardware knob. With your drum sander and a 3/4-inch square wood scrap, you can make a knob in no time.

Here's how:

Draw two layout lines surrounding your wood scrap: one 1/4 inch from the scrap's end and the other 7/8 inch from the very same end. Sand a mild concave between the lines of the layout with a 1-inch-diameter sanding drum inserted in your sander. This should be done on the knob's four sides. With a fine-toothed handsaw, chop the knob loose from the wood scrap. The knob should be made 5/8-inch long.

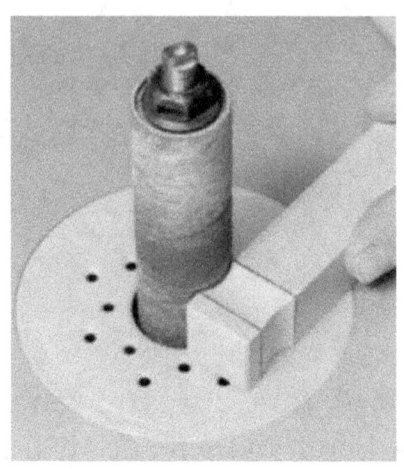

10. On the paper template, we've included a centerpoint to assist you in finding the lid's knob. Cut out the inside oval of the pattern and use an awl to mark the centerpoint on the lid's inner layers. For a #6 x 11-inch wood screw, drill a 1/8-inch diameter countersunk hole through the lid. Then, drill a stopped hole into the knob's bottom. To secure the knob, drive the screw via the lid.

11. Use your preferred finish to topcoat your box's surface, but keep the bottom of the inside bare. That way, you can add a unique touch to the bottom by lining it with colored felt. Cut the felt into the desired shape and stick it in place using glue.

Letter Jewelry Box

Materials

- Preferred wood type (18mm plywood was used here)
- Another 6mm Plywood
- Paper
- Drill Press
- Drill bit
- Scroll saw
- Sandpaper
- Finish

Additional Materials

- Wood glue
- Clamps

Instructions

1. I decided to make the size of the box the same as an A4 paper, both in height and width (297mm x 210mm). I selected my preferred font type, stretched it to fit the paper, printed it out and drew on where I needed the drawers to be, then photocopied it.

2. I cut the plywood (18mm) into four A4 size boards, then glued them together in pairs to make two 36mm thick sections. This makes cutting out

the drawer sections on the scroll saw much easier.

Allow the wood glue adhesive to dry completely. Place the two patterns on the two boards, and then use a drill press to drill a 1 mm drill bit pilot holes to feed the scroll saw blade through. Cut off the drawer sections.

After cutting all the drawer sections, use your scroll saw to cut off the box's main shape and then glue them both together.

Inspect the holes where the drawers will go to ensure they're leveled without excess glue or overhang so that the drawers can slide in smoothly, then sand the entire box to eliminate any saw marks.

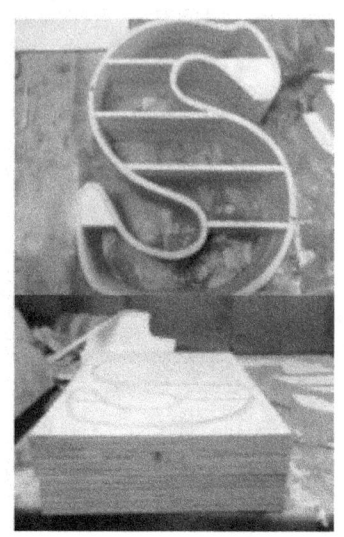

3. Now, you have two parts for each drawer. Glue and clamp them together, then wait for the glue to dry. You don't need to glue the entire piece, only the edges, because you'll be cutting a portion from it afterward.

4. Create the drawers. Remove the clamps once the glue has dried. Take a slice off the front and rear of each drawer section with the scroll saw; around 3mm or 4mm will suffice.

Now, draw on each part you want to discard to make room for a drawer. After removing a piece from each part, glue the front and rear slices back on, clamping until the glue has dried. Once they're all in place, sand them well enough and double-check that all of the drawers fit.

I cut out the left long side of a box like a letter A, not large enough to construct a drawer, and fitted some screw-in hooks to place chains or bracelets on.

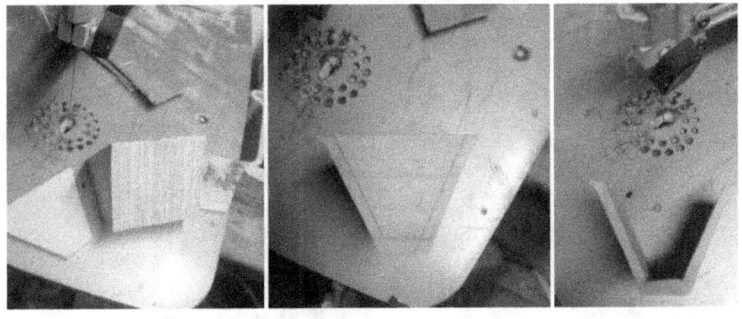

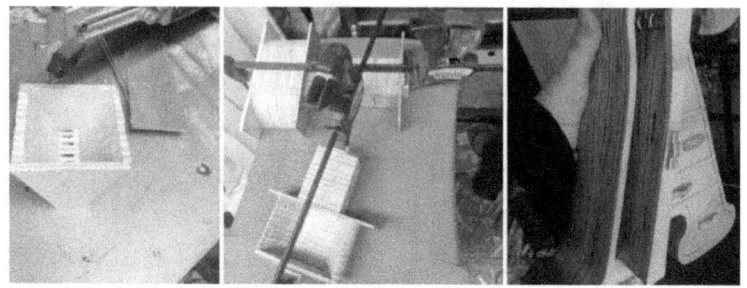

5. Make the backboard. Lay the main body of the box on a 6mm piece of plywood, trace outside the shape, then cut it out with a scroll saw. Glue and pin it in place, then sand it to ensure it's all leveled.

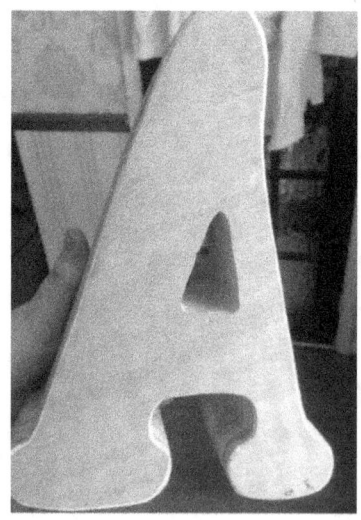

6. Cut a few handles for the drawers once you are okay with it. The same 18mm plywood was used to cut out the handles, then cut them in half, glue them on, and let them dry.

Once the handles are in place, give it a little final sanding to your satisfaction before treating the wood with a 50/50 mixture of boiled linseed oil and odorless white/mineral spirit.

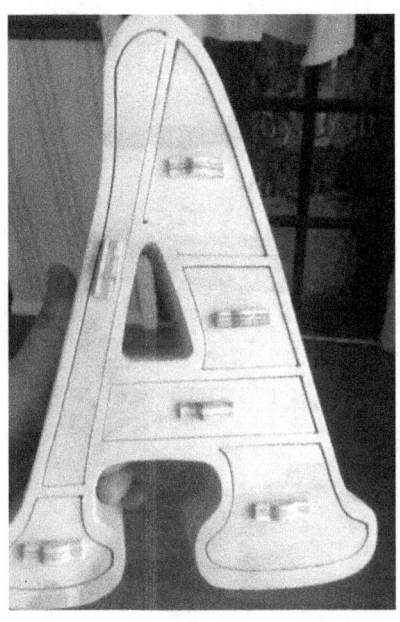

Chapter 5

Resolving Saw Scrolling Problems

When working with a scroll saw, especially as a beginner, you are bound to experience some challenges with the saw, but you can easily fix these issues with the tips you'd be learning in this section.

Let's dive into some of them and how you can troubleshoot them;

Scroll saw keeps overheating

Except you are a rookie to electric-powered tools, would you say you have no idea that virtually every electrical tool is inundated with the problem of overheating? Well, the scroll saw is not an exception. But there's a cause to it.

What is it?

You are overworking it! That's not all, even though it's the primary reason. Other issues such as material thickness, blade dullness, and wrong choice of blades are contributing factors.

To remedy this problem, first, allow the machine to cool down after working with it for a while. Do this by unplugging it from the power source and letting it cool. Other options include ensuring to use the correct blade at all times and gently handling tough materials when cutting.

After applying all of these options without success, ensure to reach out to the device manufacturer if you have a warranty or have a repairman look into it for you.

Blown fuses and tripped breakers

Your preferred electrical tool makes use of electricity and as a result, it is susceptible to blown fuses and tripped breakers. If this occurs, check your fuse box right away because the saw's functionality will be affected. Once the issue has been resolved, lower the blade speed and gradually increase it to the appropriate speed.

Turbulence of the table

Every force has an equal and opposite force, according to physics. This is also true with scroll saws. While working, your scroll saw can make the table shake, and the vibrations can be rather severe on the side of the table where the saw is positioned. To remedy this issue, choose a very clean and leveled tabletop. Better still, secure your saw to the work surface using a C clamp. The vibrations are substantially reduced as a result of this. You can, however, completely avoid this issue by purchasing a scroll saw with lower vibrations. It can be costly, but it is well worth it.

Which blade end sits atop?

It doesn't matter whether you are using a crown-tooth blade because these blades can cut in either way. The bulk of the teeth on the other type of blades should point down. Run your fingernail along the center of the blade to determine the direction of the tooth. It snags more in the teeth' direction, and if your finger is run in that direction, it feels harsher, somewhat like coarse sandpaper. Once you've determined the direction of the blade on one blade, mark the top ends of the remaining blades in the pack with a dab of inexpensive red nail polish.

The blades keep breaking

Check the tension first. The blade can snap if it is too taut and you press too hard during sawing. But, if the blade is too loose, it might catch in the wood and break as it swings from side to side. It's important to remember that tight is great, but too tight is terrible.

If the tension appears correct, but the blades continue to break, consider a larger blade.

Blades can also break because they become brittle when they heat up and lose their sharpness. Because the friction caused during the cutting operation heats the blades, grease them with beeswax or cover the blanks with tape.

Finally, dull blades are more likely to break. The best way to tell whether the blade is dull is by pressing harder to get the blade to cut or if you observe the saw cuts slowly. Because this is a gradual thing, you may not notice the dull blade until it breaks. Try replacing the blade if you observe any slow or difficult movement of the blade when you push. Several blades are often used per project; big projects or those constructed of thick or dense wood would need even more blades.

Tension fails and blades pops out occasionally from the blade holder

To avoid blades from rusting during transport, manufacturers cover them with some oil. One of the most common causes of blade slippage is oil. To clean the oil from the blade, keep a piece of sandpaper beside the saw and wipe the ends of the blade with the sandpaper before inserting it in the saw. Blades also slip when the set screws securing them become smoothly polished and stop gripping with time due to the blade's action. A little sandpaper will wipe away the polish and improve the grip of the screws.

Burning wood

Friction is caused by dull blades. Cutting any material dulls the blade, but solid wood speeds the process. The presence of burned wood indicates that the blade is dull and should be changed or that you are using the wrong blade size or type for the thickness or wood type. Not lubricating the blade with tape or wax or not lubricating the wood with a clear packing tape will cause woods such as cherry to burn. Hickory, for example, is a very hard wood that quickly dulls blades and causes burning. Also, use a bigger blade or one meant for thick or hard wood.

Lastly, burning will occur if sawdust is placed into the cut. Using a skip-tooth blade that removes sawdust as it cuts is a good option.

Blade not following the path laid out

Possible causes include under-tensioned blades, dull blades, and you may have been forcefully pushing the blade through the wood.

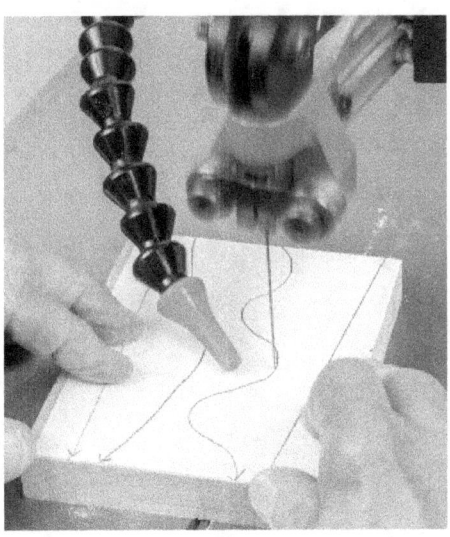

The solution is to adjust the blade's tension accordingly, replace the blade with an appropriate one, and let the blade cut at its own speed.

The cuts are not perpendicular

Possible causes include a blade that is not squared to the table, the scroller forcing the blade sideways and a blade that is under-tensioned.

Make sure the blade and table are squared; don't force the blade to cut; adjust the tension of the blade accordingly.

The blade is hard to control when cutting thin wood

Blade speed, feed rate, or either may be excessively fast are likely reasons for this problem.

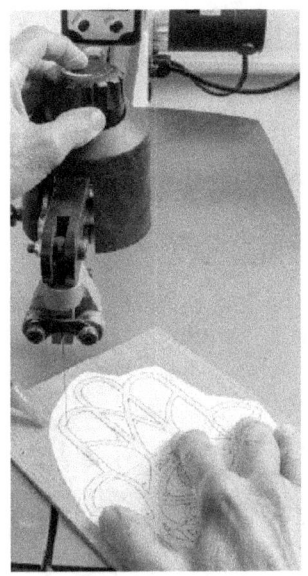

To solve this issue, reduce the speed setting and feed the wood gradually.

The workpiece bounces a lot

Possible causes include a rough workpiece or with an uneven underside or a blade positioned in an inverted manner.

To fix this issue, sand the bottom of the workpiece to make it level on the saw table, then place the blade in the proper position. To ensure proper insertion, certain blades are marked or crimped at the top.

The End... Almost!

Hey! We've made it to the final chapter of this book, and I hope you've enjoyed it so far.

If you have not done so yet, I would be incredibly thankful if you could take just a minute to leave a quick review on Amazon

Reviews are not easy to come by, and as an independent author with a little marketing budget, I rely on you, my readers, to leave a short review on Amazon.

Even if it is just a sentence or two!

So if you really enjoyed this book, please...

>> Click here to leave a brief review on Amazon.

I truly appreciate your effort to leave your review, as it truly makes a huge difference.

Chapter 6

Saw Scrolling FAQs

In this chapter, we will look at a few questions asked by scrollers. Many of your concerns have been addressed in the earlier chapters. So do ensure to go through each chapter with great attention.

Q. Is it possible to cut metal with a scroll saw blade?

Yes, many scroll saws can easily cut cold-rolled steel, copper, aluminum, and brass sheet metals.

Q. What is the difference between a scroll saw and a band saw?

An excellent band saw, despite performing the same job as a scroll saw, is significantly larger - comparable to a vending machine. Band saws are most commonly found in joinery shops. Given its size, band saws are not particularly ideal for use at home; this is where the scroll saw becomes an excellent replacement.

Q. How long will I start creating intricate shapes and designs?

153

It's tough to put a time limit on this because people learn in different ways and others have more experience than others. It's critical to remain patient and focused while meticulously tracing your outlines and using the proper blades.

If you pay attention to the details and take your time, you'll be able to look back on your early days with pride.

Q. How Do I Change a Scroll Saw Blade?

Step 1: Make sure the saw is disconnected before you begin. This is to protect you from any electrical shocks.

Step 2: Carefully remove the blade's bolts, screws, or turnable knobs. Undo the screws with the correct size of screwdriver or an Allen and wrench. The location of the screws can be seen in your device's instruction manual.

Step 3: After loosening all of the screws, detach the saw blade. With gloves on, gently detach the blade.

Step 4: After detaching the old blade, choose a new and appropriate blade. Although some modern generation blades come with teeth facing bi-direction (both up and down), the blade should be inserted with the teeth facing downwards for a cleaner cut.

Step 5: To secure the blades, identify the two holes on the new blade and align them with the holes on the old one. For securing the blade to the holder, the screws must fit into these holes.

Step 6: Tighten the screws firmly but leave room for future adjustments after positioning the new blade with the screws. To prevent any tension, make sure the blade is vertical.

Step 7: That's all there is to it! Try a cut to see if the new blade is properly installed. If necessary, tighten it even further, but be careful not to overtighten it, as this could cause the blade to strain.

Conclusion

When it comes down to whether you need a scroll saw or not, your final assessment should bolster on what you want the final result of your piece to look like. If you'd be making a 48-piece wooden puzzle, going for a jigsaw or a bandsaw would only result in an unattractive final result.

Consider the scroll saw as a complete blend of a power saw and cutting knife as elaborated in each chapter. We have looked at the scroll saw from the angle of what they are, what they can do, crafts to make profits from, the tips and techniques, and nine project ideas to get you started, among others. However, all of what we have discussed would only remain chit-chat if you don't take action on them and create those awesome works you have long desired to create. You'd be oblivious of the wonders that your scroll saw they can do unless you take action.

So, waste no further time and get busy by putting your newfound scrolling skill to work.

I wish you all the best, scroller!

www.ingramcontent.com/pod-product-compliance
Lightning Source LLC
Chambersburg PA
CBHW071152120626
46546CB00006B/2234